The Adventurous Vegetarian

Around the world in 30 meals

The Adventurous Vegetarian: Around the world in 30 meals

Published in the UK in 2013 by New Internationalist Publications Ltd
55 Rectory Road
Oxford OX4 1BW, UK
newint.org

About the author
Jane Hughes is a vegetarian food writer. Editor of *The Vegetarian* magazine since 2001, she also teaches vegetarian and vegan cookery at the Cordon Vert School and is currently Secretary of the Guild of Food Writers.

Acknowledgements
I'd like to thank John Davis of the International Vegetarian Union, Nitin Mehta of the Young Indian Vegetarians, Denis Bayomi of VegDining.com and Elisa Allen of PETA UK for their enthusiastic support of this project and for helping me to make contact with vegetarians and vegans all over the world. Heartfelt thanks to everybody who contributed recipes and ideas – the book wouldn't have worked without you and it was lovely to 'meet' so many brilliant vegetarian campaigners and cooks. Thanks to Dan and Chris at New Internationalist for their gentle guidance, and to Graham for the lovely photos.
Last but far from least, my family, especially Gwilym for his patience and for driving up and down the motorway in the middle of the night, and Mum and Keith, for letting me take over their kitchen when I was cooking for photo shoots and for helping with the washing up.

Design: Ian Nixon
Food photography: Graham Alder/MM Studios
For other photographs' credits, see page 286.

Printed by 1010 Printing International Ltd, who hold environmental accreditation ISO 14001.

British Library Cataloguing-in-Publication Data
A catalogue record for this book is available from the British Library.

Library of Congress Cataloging-in-Publication Data
A catalog record for this book is available from the Library of Congress.

Hardback ISBN 978-1-78026-160-7
Paperback ISBN 978-1-78026-124-9

The Adventurous Vegetarian

Around the world in 30 meals

JANE HUGHES

CONTENTS

The Adventurous Vegetarian

Around the world in 30 meals

CONTENTS

Introduction

Do you think you know vegetarian cuisine? Think again. It's easy to imagine that vegetarian food can be defined, and that it has a certain style – like Chinese food, Indian food, Mexican food. But vegetarianism is different, because it has no boundaries.

Vegetarianism is a worldwide phenomenon. In the UK (and in many other parts of the world, including cities like Sao Paolo, Cape Town and Los Angeles), we have Meat Free Mondays, but Ghent, in Belgium, was the first city to introduce a meat-free day (Thursdays) and in Denmark there is a campaign for Kod-fri Fredag – Meat-free Fridays. Wherever a thoughtful cook realizes that a meat-based diet is ultimately unsustainable, and sees the damage that over-reliance on meat does to our environment and to our health, there's an impulse to take the food they know and make it better.

All over the world, people are building on the culinary history of their country, making the most of the fresh produce that grows around them, and making their food vegetarian or vegan. Every style of eating can be veggified, whether it's a curry, a stir-fry or a barbecue. Wherever vegetarians are in the world, we are part of a global community with shared principles, and yet we're all eating differently. The idea behind this book was to make it possible for vegetarians, wherever they may be, to sit down to a meal similar to that which might be on the table in a vegetarian household on the other side of the world. It's about the kind of food that people eat every day, and it's about sharing.

Having been associated with the Vegetarian Society UK for many years, as the editor of *The Vegetarian* magazine and a tutor at the Cordon Vert Cookery School, I was able to contact friendly people at the International Vegetarian Union, the Young Indian Vegetarians and PETA, who in turn had vegetarian and vegan friends all over the world who were willing to share

their recipes. My job was to test each recipe in my own kitchen, to iron out any really challenging techniques, and to find workable alternatives where recipes used ingredients that were really hard to come by. This doesn't mean that I've taken the recipes and westernized them dramatically, or made them easy – to have done so would have taken a good deal of the adventure out of the book!

Although some of the chapter introductions include tips about finding vegetarian and vegan food if you should visit the country concerned, this is not really a book for travelers – instead, it's about letting the world come to you, and inviting vegetarians from across the globe into your kitchen to share a meal. What better way to celebrate the fact that there are vegetarians all over the world?

Some of the recipes are easy: the Chinese ABC soup and Egyptian spiced oranges, for example, are both favorites in my household now. But I must admit that I enjoy a culinary challenge, and there are lots of new tastes and techniques to try here. If, like me, you have an adventurous approach to cooking, then you'll love making your own ghee and paneer, and roasting and grinding complex Ethiopian spice mixtures. You'll relish the challenge of making an omelet 'net', and tackle the fiddly job of making 'Torn Underwear Cookies' with gusto.

I am an experienced cook, but there are always new ideas and techniques to learn. I was surprised when I tried the Botswanan Potjie recipe, which involves cooking a mountain of vegetables in a splash of water on a very low heat for 90 minutes. It works. Oildown, the national dish of Grenada, was another revelation. A selection of Caribbean root vegetables is cooked slowly in coconut milk: the watery part of the 'milk' seeps into the veg, while the oily part gently rises to the top of the pot, coating every piece of veg as it ascends. Perhaps that's not the best recipe to choose if you're trying to lose weight! Another naughty but nice dish is the spiced Lebanese potato kibbeh, which is drenched with oil when it goes into the oven, but miraculously both crispy and gooey when it comes out.

Some of these recipes provide the perfect excuse to rummage in shops that specialize in produce from the Far East, the Caribbean or India. It's all part of the adventure! These recipes will show you how to use pandan essence, palm sugar, Lebanese 7-spice and preserved lemons. Try to get them if you can – using authentic ingredients is the only way to get authentic flavors. If all else fails, it's amazing what you can buy via the internet these days.

But it's not all about strange ingredients. Naturally, I cook and eat rice quite regularly – and rice is synonymous with 'fluffy'. I'd certainly never cooked it to a mush, attacked it with a potato masher and patted it into sticky balls to float on a bowl of soup – or put it into a food processor with a handful of aromatic herbs and whizzed it into a dough! Peanut butter is for making sandwiches – I hadn't considered using it to thicken a soup or a stew – but what a perfect way to boost the protein content of a vegetable dish.

In one or two instances, I've resorted to inventing new dishes to give a flavor of a country's authentic cuisine where there are very few existing vegetarian dishes to try. Kirsten Skaarup, a prolific Danish vegetarian cookery writer and blogger, gently explained to me that Denmark has no history of vegetarian food, so her healthy plant-based recipes are purely her own invention. Similarly, Tobias Leenaert of the Belgian vegetarian organization, EVA (Ethical

Vegetarian Alternative), told me that audiences at his talks and cookery demonstrations in Ghent were unable to think of any vegetarian dishes that they had grown up with. The EVA has worked hard to create vegetarian and vegan-friendly versions of Belgian classics, like the hearty beer stew with chunky seitan that they contributed to this book.

Erick Mokafo-Brhom Yeleneke sent instructions for making fufu by pounding yams, a daily activity in Togo but not something that translated well to the Western kitchen. I compromised with polenta and created a tasty vegan version of a chicken dish which I have named Togo Tofu. Australia presented difficulties too – the traditional national diet is very meaty. I created some beetroot burgers, which are authentically pink and packed with chewy quinoa – very satisfactory on the barbie. For a final flourish, I decided upon Lamingtons, a very traditional Aussie cake named after Baron Lamington, governor of Queensland from 1896 to 1901 (or possibly named after his hat). I'll bet he never expected his cakes to be veganized!

I had a lot of fun exploring international vegetarian cuisine and it's wonderful to have the chance to share what I've learned. I found out how to make avocado ice cream and Indian pistachio kulfi, and what mojo means to the Chileans, and as well as broadening my personal repertoire of dishes, I now have a far better understanding of what vegetarianism really means to people in different countries. Whether you're an experienced vegetarian cook looking for fresh inspiration, or you're just starting out and experimenting with occasional meat-free dishes, I hope you'll get as much fun out of these recipes and menu plans as I did.

Jane Hughes

Australia

Think of Australian food and you're likely to think of barbecues and campfires. This passion for outdoor eating (and penchant for meat) may have its roots in the habits of the earliest settlers – and in Aboriginal culture before that. Although the Aboriginal diet is thought to have been 80-90% plant-based, wild animals like possums, koalas, flying foxes, small rodents and lizards, as well as insects, birds and fish of all kinds, all contributed.

The first British penal colony was established in 1788, and by 1840 there were several more, along with a 'free-settler' colony in South Australia. The voyage from Britain took between three and six months, during which time the travelers had no option but to live on rations of dry bread and salted meat, along with some cheese, oatmeal and dried peas. Things didn't improve much when they arrived – there was no agriculture to speak of, and the convicts and guards who arrived in the earliest ships were forced to continue to live on the same diet, supplemented with supplies from each new ship to arrive.

Attempts by early settlers to farm in the same way as they had done at home were doomed to failure and a lasting reliance on imported food developed. The best way to use the land seemed to be to farm sheep – not primarily for their meat, but for their wool, which was a valuable commodity for export. Meat was a cheap by-product of the industry and was consumed in large amounts at every meal. It would not become possible to export meat until the advent of refrigerated shipping in the 1870s.

Shepherds and sheep-shearers were partially paid in spirits and food, generally a weekly ration that came to be known as 'ten, ten, two and a quarter' – ten pounds of flour, ten pounds of meat, two pounds of sugar and a quarter pound of tea, plus salt. The meat (mutton,

corned beef or salted meat) could be cooked over an open fire, and the flour mixed with water to make a rudimentary bread called a damper, which was cooked in the ashes of the fire. This cheap, satisfying and simple way of eating was widely adopted by other groups of men who worked outdoors for low wages: construction workers, railway and road builders, sailors and soldiers. At the same time, middle-class folk with aspirations to a genteel lifestyle styled their meals on British Victorian conventions as far as they could.

The habit of gathering around an open fire to eat meat and drink alcohol isn't one that the Australians look likely to give up in a hurry. But these days, there are vegetarian and vegan organizations all over the country. Brian Loffler, from New Internationalist's Australian office, writes: 'My impression is that vegetarian fare is easy to come by; there are plenty of restaurants and cafés that specialize in good tasty vegetarian food. I don't think it's difficult to be a vegetarian in Australia, nor does it invite criticism. That's been a huge change over the past few decades. Back in the 1950s, meat and three veg was the standard meal. Thanks to many immigrants from Asia, Africa and Latin America, that monoculture has changed dramatically and we now have a super range of choices. Urban Spoon – the iPhone App – indicates there are 59 vegetarian restaurants and cafés near me in Adelaide and its surrounds, which I think is quite good for a modestly sized city.'

Many of Australia's vegetarian and vegan groups have useful websites, with lists of restaurants and tips for visitors.

Australian Vegetarian Society **veg-soc.org**

Vegetarian Society of South Australia **vegsa.org.au**

Vegetarian/Vegan Society of Queensland **vegsoc.org.au**

Vegan Society of New South Wales
vegansocietynsw.com

AUSTRALIA

Asparagus and macadamia nut salad

Macadamia nuts are native to Australia and are the only native plant product that is grown for export in any quantity. They're quite large, soft nuts and are widely available in supermarkets. Oddly, they are toxic to dogs, so take care if you are a pet owner.

Ingredients

A bunch of asparagus

A handful of macadamia nuts

Cherry tomatoes

2 cups / 250 g feta cheese

¼ cup / 60 ml olive oil, plus extra for cooking

Juice of ½ lemon

2 cloves garlic, crushed

Salt and pepper to taste

Method

Preheat the oven to 375°F/190°C. Trim the asparagus and put it into an ovenproof dish. Drizzle with olive oil and cook for between 10 and 20 minutes (depending on the thickness of the asparagus spears). Allow to cool.

Put the macadamia nuts into a dry, heavy-bottomed pan and toast them over a medium heat for 2-3 minutes until beginning to color. Tip them onto a cool plate to halt the cooking process.

Cut the tomatoes into halves and crumble the feta. Make the salad dressing by whisking the olive oil, lemon juice, garlic and salt and pepper together. Arrange the asparagus on a serving platter or individual plates. Add the tomatoes and feta, and drizzle with the dressing.

AUSTRALIA

Beetroot burgers

Veggie burgers are standard fare for vegetarians at barbecues, and nobody barbies like the Aussies! I invented this version when I found out that, unlike practically everybody else, Australians like to slip a slice of pickled beetroot between their burger and their bun. This one builds in the beetroot along with some high protein quinoa which gives them a really firm and 'meaty' texture. The general 'meatiness' is also played up by the rich color of the beetroot. I shallow-fried mine and then transferred them to a griddle pan to give them some lovely smoky black stripes.

Ingredients

¾ cup / 150 g red or white quinoa

2 beetroots

1 large carrot

1 onion

2 cloves garlic

3 eggs

⅔ cup / 100 g plain white flour

½ tsp fennel seeds

½ tsp salt

Method

Put the quinoa into a saucepan, cover with water, bring to the boil and simmer for around 12 minutes until just tender. Drain and set aside to cool.

Trim, peel and grate the beetroot and the carrot. Chop the onion finely, crush the garlic and beat the eggs. Put all the ingredients into a large bowl and mix together thoroughly.

Shape the mixture into small patties and shallow-fry gently in a little vegetable oil. If you want to put them onto a barbecue, it's best to fry them first, to firm them up, and then reheat them on the hot grill. If you like stripes on your burgers, brush the fried burgers with a little more vegetable oil and transfer them to a preheated griddle pan. Letting them sit on the hot ridges of the pan gives them the stripes, so don't be tempted to move them around – and be prepared for a bit of a smoky kitchen!

Perfect in a toasted burger bun with all the usual trimmings.

Lamingtons

Lamingtons are much-loved traditional cakes in Australia, and have graced Australian teatimes since the turn of the last century. The story behind them varies – some say they were named after Baron Lamington, governor of Queensland from 1896 to 1901. Some say they were invented in honor of his wife. Some say they were called Lamingtons because they resembled the governor's hat. Whatever the reason, Lamingtons are simply delicious and that's why they have survived into the 21st century. You can make these with a ready-made vanilla sponge cake or a Madeira cake, but take care not to choose anything too soft or crumbly as it may disintegrate when you try to dip it into the chocolate icing. This is a vegan version.

Ingredients

For the sponge cake:

2 cups / 200 g white self-rising flour

3 tsp baking powder

¼ cup plus ⅓ cup / 115 g sugar

½ cup / 125 ml vegetable oil

1⅓ cups / 325 ml cold water

2 tsp vanilla essence

For the icing:

4 cups / 500 g icing sugar

⅓ cup / 40 g cocoa powder

2 tsp vegan margarine

½ cup / 120 ml soya milk

½ lb / 225 g desiccated coconut

Method

Preheat oven to 375°F/190°C.

Mix all the cake ingredients together thoroughly and pour into a greased and lined rectangular tin. Bake for 35 minutes or until a skewer inserted into the middle of the cake comes out clean. Allow to cool, then cut into squares. The size of the cakes is your choice but I kept mine quite small – around 2½ inches / 6 cm square.

Bring a little water to simmering point in a large saucepan. Sift the icing sugar and cocoa together in a large heat-proof bowl. Stir in the soya milk and margarine, and place the bowl on top of the saucepan. Stir the mixture over the heat until it melts to form a thick, glossy icing.

Stick a fork into one of the pieces of cake and dip it into the warm icing so that every side is covered. Lift it up to drain off any excess icing and transfer to a tray lined with baking parchment. Sprinkle the cake with desiccated coconut while it is still wet. Repeat with all of the remaining cakes and transfer the tray to the refrigerator to allow them to cool and set.

Belgium

Tobias Leenaert is the Director of the Belgian vegetarian organization, EVA (Ethical Vegetarian Alternative). Tobias and his colleague Maureen Vande Cappelle kindly supplied these recipes. Tobias writes:

Belgium is almost two countries: Flanders (Dutch speaking) in the North, and Wallonia (French speaking) in the south. The language border is also a border for vegetarianism. In the north of Belgium (and in Scandinavia, the UK, the Netherlands and Germany) I should say that things are not too bad for vegetarians. In the south of Belgium (and France, Spain and Italy), options for vegetarians are fewer.

In Belgium, as in the rest of Europe, veganism and vegetarianism are not synonymous. In the US, many more vegetarians are actually vegans than is the case in Europe. In Belgium, veganism is considered an extreme and unusual version of vegetarianism.

Belgium doesn't have many vegetarian dishes in its culinary repertoire. Indeed, whenever we ask our audience, during presentations, if anybody can come up with a real vegetarian main dish which has been passed down through their family, people go blank. That's not something you would see in many other countries – so yes, there are challenges for vegetarians here.

Cities are obviously the best places to get vegetarian food,

and amongst those, the place to be is Ghent, which has probably
the highest per capita number of vegetarian restaurants (13 for
a population of 240,000) of any Western city that we know of.
We're not exactly sure why that is, but it's the most progressive town
in Belgium, with a very high student population (about 70,000 students). It's also the town
where the Belgian vegetarian organization EVA (Ethical Vegetarian Alternative) has its offices.
Ghent attracted worldwide press attention when it became the first city in the world officially
to institute a weekly vegetarian day (which is not to say you wouldn't see anyone eating meat
on Thursdays…). Belgium has a small chain of organic supermarkets called Bio-Planet, and
many smaller organic stores. They provide the best selection of meat substitutes and other
vegetarian foods, though the range available in supermarkets is increasing.

There's no real national vegetarian dish, although some people manage to stir up quite good
imitations of traditional meat dishes. Stoverij, for instance, is a beer stew traditionally made
with beef. Vegetarians make it with seitan, a wheat product which seems to be more easily
available here than in other countries. It is typically served with Belgian fries (which,
make no mistake, are mostly cooked in lard when you buy them at the typical
frietkot or fries place).

evavzw.be

BELGIUM

Chicory soup

Ingredients

2 onions

$\frac{1}{3}$ cup / 50 g margarine

18 oz / 500 g chicory

2 tsp sugar

1 cup / 250 ml soy milk

4 cups / 1 litre water

Salt and pepper

Fresh parsley, to garnish

Method

Chop the onions finely and, in a large pan, fry them in the margarine until they are soft and translucent. Chop the chicory and add it to the pan along with the sugar. Continue to cook, stirring frequently, until the chicory is lightly browned. Pour in the soy milk and the water, bring the soup to the boil, check that the chicory is cooked through and season to taste with salt and pepper. Garnish with finely chopped parsley to serve.

BELGIUM

Belgian beer stew

Tobias writes: 'This is a vegan version of a traditional recipe from Ghent, but there are many varieties in Belgium.' Seitan is a surprisingly realistic meat substitute made from wheat gluten. It's readily available in Belgian health-food shops but is not always easy to find in other countries, where you could use a more available meat substitute. There are several particularly Belgian ingredients in this dish. Tobias recommends the traditional Tierentyn mustard which is made in Ghent – if you can't get any, use a good quality medium-strength variety. The gingerbread should really be a traditional Belgian *peperkoek* – but a good quality ginger cake will do. There is no substitute, however, for authentic brown Belgian beer in this recipe – Tobias mentions Gruut, which is from Ghent, Piedbeuf and Westmalle II. If you can't get a sweet brown *abdijbier* ('abbey beer') like these, don't make this dish – it wouldn't be the same without it!

Ingredients

2 tbsp olive oil	2 tbsp mustard
2 onions	1²⁄₃ cups / 400 ml vegetable stock
1 pound / 450 g seitan	1 pint / ½ litre Belgian brown beer
2 bay leaves	2 slices of gingerbread
1 tbsp mixed dried herbs	Brown sugar to taste
1 slice bread	Salt and pepper to taste

Method

If you're using fresh, unflavored seitan, cut it into chunks and fry it gently in a little oil for a few minutes, to firm it up and give it more flavor.

Chop the onions and, in a large, deep saucepan, fry them in the olive oil until soft and translucent. Stir in the seitan, dried herbs and bay leaves, then pour in the vegetable stock. Spread the mustard onto the bread and add this to the mixture. As it disintegrates it will help to thicken the stew. Simmer the stew on a very low heat for an hour – you can also do this the day before you want to eat the stew, as letting the ingredients blend overnight improves the flavor.

Add the beer and crumbled gingerbread and simmer, uncovered, until the cake melts into the mixture. Season with salt and pepper – add a little brown sugar if you like a sweeter taste.

The stew is traditionally served with fries, apple sauce, mayonnaise and a simple green salad.

BELGIUM

Apple crumble pie

This recipe calls for a box of the traditional Belgian ginger biscuits called *speculoos*. If you can't get them, any crisp ginger biscuits should work. It's amazing to see how they soak up the apple juice as this dish cooks, to form a delicious dark, gingery layer in the bottom of the pie.

Ingredients

1 sheet of ready-rolled puff pastry

9 oz / 250 g ginger biscuits

5 cooking apples

4 cups / 600 g cold margarine

½ cup / 90 g brown sugar

1¼ cups / 125 g plain white flour

Apple sauce, Belgian apple syrup or quince jelly

Flaked almonds

Method

Preheat the oven to 355°F/180°C. Put the pastry into the base of a deep, oven-proof dish and prick it with a fork. Cover it with a layer of ginger biscuits and brush generously with apple sauce, Belgian apple syrup or quince jelly.

Make the crumble topping: rub the margarine into the flour and then mix in the sugar.

Peel, core and slice the apples. Arrange them in the pie dish and top with the crumble mixture. Bake the pie for 35 minutes, then remove from the oven, sprinkle with flaked almonds and bake for a further 10 minutes until golden.

Botswana

Vegetarianism is rare in Botswana. Most meals contain meat, beef being the most popular and plentiful option, and, even in the poorest rural areas, families keep animals which are slaughtered for food on special occasions. For more everyday protein, many families rely on large grubs called mopane worms. Botswana does not have a coastline but river fish are a significant part of the diet. Maize and sorghum are widely grown, along with many varieties of bean and vegetables, and the cuisine also draws upon the seasonal availability of wild foods, including wild melons, which have evolved to survive the arid desert conditions that dominate 70% of the country. Watermelons are believed to have originated in Botswana, and these are cheap and abundant in season. Situated immediately north of South Africa, the country is very central and the cuisine is influenced by the countries to the south, east and west. The country occupies a key position for trade, and foodstuffs that are not grown can often be imported from neighboring countries.

Legodile Seganabeng is a Botswanan vegetarian and he writes about his experience.

As I grew up, in an archetypal African extended family, I never knew I'd one day become a vegetarian. I didn't know there was such a thing as vegetarianism. I was raised in a strongly "carnivorous" society where a meal without meat was deemed incomplete and not at all desirable.

My family's basic sustenance depended on both livestock keeping and seasonal crop farming. We also kept home-grown, free-range chickens. Unlike the goats and cattle that were kept far away at the farm, the chickens lived with us. They mingled with us in our day-to-day lives. They were like pets; like the dog and the cat. But unlike the dog and the cat, chickens in my family were kept solely for their meat. Occasionally, a chicken would go into a pot and a meal with chicken was one of the most prestigious. When an important visitor came, a chicken lost its life.

In my early twenties, I went to study in a South African university. One day in Johannesburg, I saw a magazine advert for vegetarian burgers and

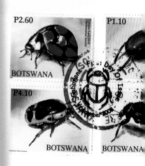

sausages. The tag-line was: 'No animals were hurt in the preparation of this meal'. This line caught my attention. It made me think hard. I realized that my consumption of meat contributed to the hurting and ultimate killing of sentient beings. I also came to realize, through research, that the production of meat can be environmentally unsustainable and thus affect ecology and the environment. I changed my diet. I didn't stop eating meat for religious and health purposes only. I felt for the animals and wanted to help stop their suffering.

It wasn't easy for me to become a complete vegetarian straight away. I gradually cut out meat, then fish and eggs. Although I am still eating dairy products at the moment, I intend to go completely vegan eventually.

Most of my flesh-eating friends feel sorry for me, because I'm vegetarian. They see vegetarianism as a difficult choice. In my society, the most common plate consists of pap *(maize-meal porridge),* morogo *(leafy greens, such as spinach) and, of course, meat. The* morogo *is an option – you can have a meal without it and it will still be fine. But a meal with just pap and* morogo *is considered unbalanced, with very little nutrition. Of course, vegetarians needn't be limited to those foods! But being vegetarian in a community like this is a challenge. Most restaurants in towns don't offer vegetarian options and eating out isn't something to look forward to. I never really trust what someone else has cooked, unless I've seen them cook it.*

Legodile Seganabeng hails from the village of Tonota, Botswana. He is a published writer, spoken word performer, recorded poet and practicing fine artist. He won the Bessie Head Literature Award in 2010.

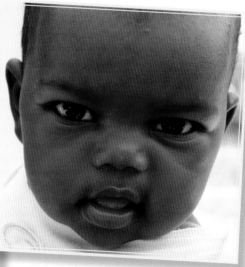

BOTSWANA

Watermelon and tomato salad

Ingredients

3 or 4 small tomatoes (in a mixture of colors if possible), cut into chunks

1 small cucumber, peeled, seeded and cut into chunks

1 cup / 125 g seedless watermelon flesh, cut into chunks

1 avocado, peeled, stoned and cut into chunks

1 tbsp fresh chopped herbs (any combination of basil, tarragon, chives and fresh cilantro/coriander)

¼ tsp ground coriander

3 tbsp olive oil

3 tbsp balsamic vinegar

Salt and black pepper

Method

Mix all the chopped fruit, vegetables, fresh herbs and ground coriander together in a large bowl. Make the dressing by combining the oil, vinegar and seasoning. Toss the dressing through the salad and serve immediately.

BOTSWANA

Vegetable potjie

Potjie is an Afrikaans word that translates as 'pottage'. Like many old-fashioned African dishes, this is designed to cook for a long time over a relatively low heat. Rather than simmering in the stock, the vegetables are steamed – so although the mixture seems dry to start with, if you cover it and leave it for 90 minutes, all the vegetables will be tender. The sweetcorn can be fresh, canned or frozen.

Ingredients

½ pound / 225 g potatoes

1 pound / 450 g butternut squash

2 large carrots

1 cup / 125 g sweetcorn kernels

1 small turnip

1 stick of celery

⅓ cup / 80 ml vegetable oil

3 onions

6 cloves of garlic

1 tsp salt

Black pepper to taste

2 tsp dried oregano

2 tsp dried basil

1 cup / 240 ml vegetable stock

Method

Peel the vegetables and cut them into bite-sized pieces. Cut the sweetcorn kernels off the cobs. Heat the oil in a large lidded saucepan. Fry the onions until they begin to soften, then add the garlic and cook for a further minute. Layer the chopped vegetables on top, and sprinkle with the herbs, salt and pepper. Pour the stock into the pan, cover and simmer on a very low heat for 90 minutes until all the vegetables are tender.

Diphaphatha (fried bread)

A traditional fried bread to serve with your potjie.

Ingredients

4 cups / 400 g self-rising white flour

Pinch of salt

1 tsp sugar

1¼ cups / 300 ml milk

Method

Put all the ingredients into a large bowl, mix well and then turn out onto a floured board and knead to make a firm dough. Use a rolling pin to roll the dough out to about ¼ inch / ½ cm thick and then cut into circles around 3 inches / 8cm in diameter.

Heat a large, heavy frying pan. Cook the dough circles on a very low heat, without oil, for about 10 minutes on each side – they should puff up a little to make small, plain, versatile breads.

BOTSWANA

West African ginger beer

Desserts are not particularly popular or widely consumed in Botswana – a slice of watermelon does the job. Refreshing home-made non-alcoholic ginger beer is very popular and enjoyed all over Western and Central Africa.

Ingredients

25 oz / 700 g root ginger

Juice of 2 limes or lemons

1 cup / 200 g granulated sugar

Cinnamon stick or cloves, optional

Method

Traditionally, the ginger root is pounded to a pulp. Grating it will work too, and there is no need to peel it first. Put it into a large heat-proof bowl, along with any juice that appears while you are grating it, and pour 3 pints / 1.5 litres of boiling water over it. Cover the bowl and leave it in a warm place – a sunny windowsill or on top of the oven. (If all else fails, put it into a large saucepan, warm it up a little and then remove from the heat.) Leave to steep for an hour, then strain the liquid through a muslin cloth. Pour the liquid into a large measuring jug and add the lime or lemon juice and the sugar, stirring well to make sure it dissolves. Many people like to add a few cloves or a stick of cinnamon at this point – everybody has their own preference! Top up the liquid to 4 pints / 2 litres, and return it to the warm spot, covered, for a further hour. Finally, remove the spices if you have used any and decant the cordial into screw-top bottles. Chill and serve over ice, or diluted with cold water.

Brazil

Brazil is the fifth-largest country in the world, with a mainly tropical climate. It was a Portuguese colony from 1500 until achieving independence in 1822, with a short period of Spanish rule in the late 16th century. Though it is home to a huge population, the overall population density is low, with most people living in the cosmopolitan cities along the coastline. Around 57 per cent of the land is covered by the Amazonian rainforest. The rainforest is being cleared at a rate of around 20,000 square miles / 32,000 square kilometres per year – first, for its valuable timber, and second, for farming and cattle grazing land.

In the West, Brazilian food is barely understood, and is represented only by *churrascarias* – 'all you can eat' meat restaurants. But Brazilians enjoy a bounty of native produce. It is thought that at least 3,000 different species of fruit grow in the rainforest; the indigenous peoples who live there use about 2,000 varieties. Only about 200 are used in the West – avocados, coconuts, bananas, guavas, figs, oranges, lemons, grapefruit, pineapples, mangoes, acerolas and acai berries all originated in the rainforest, not to mention spices (cinnamon, cloves, cayenne, turmeric, black pepper, ginger) and favorites like vanilla, cashews, sugar cane, pine nuts, coffee, Brazil nuts, guarana and chocolate.

But there are so many more that have yet to become well known outside the country: strawberry guavas, rumberries, hog plums... It has been argued that keeping the rainforest ecosystem intact and harvesting its edible plants, oil-producing plants and medicinal plants would create a far greater (and more sustainable) income for landowners than mowing down the timber and using the land for cattle ranching. Creating sufficient worldwide demand for these rainforest products would help to halt rainforest destruction for short-term gain.

Manioc, rice, beans, okra, peanuts and fresh tropical fruit are prevalent in the national diet, but there are regional variations, with Portuguese and African influences (a legacy of the Atlantic slave trade) detectable in the food enjoyed in the north of the country. German and

MENU

Vegetable maionese salad

•

Brown rice tart

•

Guava sorbet with pomegranate syrup

Italian settlers gave the south a taste for red meat, wine and pasta. Vegetarianism is rare, with meat or fish a part of most meals. A mixture of rice and beans is also commonly served with most meals, but this is far from a safe option for vegetarians as it's often made with lard or pork fat. In the cities, the best options might be serve-yourself 'kilo' restaurants, falafel stands, cheesebread (*pao de queijo*) and spaghetti. The Brazilians love desserts and all kinds of sweets and cakes are made with the fruit, nuts and chocolate that are native to the country. Interestingly, Brazilians consider eating with the hands to be unhygienic and are inclined to tackle even slices of pizza, pieces of fruit and sandwiches with a knife and fork.

Marly Winckler, the President of the Brazilian vegetarian society (Sociedade Vegetariana Brasileira, svb.org.br) is currently Chair of the International Council of the IVU (International Vegetarian Union), and has devoted a great deal of her time to managing online resources for vegetarians and organizing vegetarian conferences both inside and outside Brazil. The SVB is currently celebrating its 10th birthday and has 15 campaigning groups across the country. Marly put me in touch with Luana Budel, who lectures on gastronomy in São Paulo, and Marta Tatini, a vegan eco-chef. The recipes they kindly supplied made use of vegetables and fruit that were completely unfamiliar to me!

Luana has websites at **wix.com/abobrinhas/catering** and **falandoaborinhas.com.br**

Marta's website is at **taiobagastronomia.com**

Vegetable maionese salad

Marta's vegan variation of this very typical mayonnaise salad included cooked, puréed arracacha as the main ingredient. Various internet sources explained that this is an Andean root vegetable somewhere between a carrot and celery. As celery, to my mind, is more of a green stem than a root, I was none the wiser – perhaps they meant celeriac, but the idea of pureed celeriac in mayonnaise wasn't too appealing. I've Westernized the ingredients, but the mayo is still home-made and vegan.

Ingredients

4 potatoes

2 carrots

4 oz / 110 g green beans

4 oz / 110 g fresh or defrosted frozen peas

3 oz / 75 g stoned olives

½ 14-oz / 400-g can hearts of palm

Approx 1 cup / 250 ml vegan mayonnaise

For the mayonnaise:

5 tbsp chilled soya milk

1½ tbsp fresh lemon juice, chilled

¾ cup / 175 ml light vegetable oil

Salt and pepper, to taste

Method

Make the mayonnaise first. It's important that the soya milk and lemon juice are chilled. Put them into a goblet blender, season with salt and pepper, put the lid on and start the motor running. Very slowly drizzle the oil into the blender – there should be a little hole in the lid to enable you to do this – it's the standard technique for making mayonnaise. Eventually the mayo will emulsify and thicken, and you'll notice a change in the sound of the motor as the blades encounter more resistance.

The potatoes, carrots, beans and peas all need to be cooked and cooled before the salad is assembled (which means it's a good way to use up leftovers!). Peel the potatoes and carrots, dice them and cook them in boiling salted water until they are tender. Trim the beans, chop them into short lengths and cook them, and the peas, the same way.

Drain the hearts of palm and slice them. Slice the olives – you can just halve them or leave them whole, but slices look prettier.

Put all the prepared vegetables into a large mixing bowl and stir in sufficient mayonnaise to coat everything well. Serve chilled.

BRAZIL

Brown rice tart

Marta suggested topping this tart with taro leaves, sugar beet stalks and edible flowers. I have tried to do justice to her recipe with a colorful combination of red endive, carrots, purple sprouting broccoli, red onions, ruby chard and beetroot stalks.

Ingredients

7 oz / 200 g organic brown long grain rice

1 cup / 250 ml vegetable stock

½ cup / 125 ml sunflower oil

1 tbsp baking powder

Gersalt (salt with sesame seeds) or sea salt to taste

Fresh herbs (chives, basil, rosemary or oregano) to taste

A colorful selection of stems and leaves (try baby carrots, sprouting broccoli, endive, spring onions, red onions, beetroot stems, ruby chard)

2-3 tbsp olive oil

Method

Cook the rice in a pan of boiling water until it is just tender – then drain and leave to cool. Preheat the oven to 350°F /180°C. Use a food processor to blend the cooked rice with the stock, oil, baking powder, salt and fresh herbs, if you want to use any. Line a deep roasting tin with baking parchment and grease the sides. Spoon the rice mixture into the tin, smooth the top and make sure every corner is filled.

Wash and trim your chosen topping ingredients, cutting any chunky ones into slices, and sauté them in the olive oil for 2-3 minutes – the purpose is not to cook them but to make sure they are sealed with oil which will help them to roast, and not dry out, in the oven. Spread the topping over the rice base and bake for approximately 20 minutes until the base is cooked through. Serve immediately.

BRAZIL

Guava sorbet with pomegranate syrup

Luana made this with red guavas, peeled and puréed in a blender. After a fruitless (sorry) search, I compromised with guava juice, which made a delicious sweet sorbet that really melted in the mouth – using a purée of ripe peaches might also be good. If you're seeking the wow factor, try your hand at making sugar baskets or sugar cages to serve with the sorbet – it's not difficult once you get the hang of it and even if it all goes wrong, you should end up with some pretty sugar shards to decorate your dessert!

Ingredients

8 tbsp organic Demerara sugar

5 peeled red guavas (or 3 cups / 750 ml guava juice)

1½ cups / 375 ml orange juice

Organic pomegranate syrup, to taste

For the sugar baskets:

8 tbsp granulated white sugar

Method

Mix the Demerara sugar with the orange juice until it dissolves. If you're using whole guavas or peaches, peel and chop the flesh, and put it into a blender with the sweetened orange juice. Blend until smooth, then pass the mixture through a sieve. If you're using guava juice, just mix it with the sweetened orange juice. Put the mixture into an ice-cream maker and freeze according to the manufacturer's instructions. (I wouldn't recommend making this without a machine – it really needs to be churned as it freezes, otherwise it will turn into a very solid, icy block.) Serve as soon as it reaches a firm consistency, with a drizzle of pomegranate syrup.

To make sugar baskets: Grease a small heat-proof bowl with a little vegetable oil and stand it upside down on a large sheet of baking parchment. Put the sugar into a heavy-bottomed pan and melt it over a low heat. Don't rush it – if it gets too hot it will bubble up and burn. Use a metal spoon to stir the melted sugar and keep it on a very low heat. Take a spoonful of melted sugar, lift it high over the pan and slowly pour the sugar back down into the pan. Keep doing this – at first the sugar will be very liquid, but eventually you will notice that as it falls, it starts to solidify in mid-air, making very fine filaments. This is the point when you can begin to drizzle the melted sugar over the upturned greased bowl – drizzle the sugar syrup from a height, and move the spoon from side to side over the bowl. You'll need to work very quickly – if the sugar cools down too much, the filaments will crack in midair and eventually the mixture will start falling off the spoon in big unsightly blobs. If this happens, carefully reheat the sugar and repeat the pouring process until it reaches the filament stage again. Once your bowl is covered with sugar strands, it will not be long before the sugar is cool and solid enough to be lifted off the bowl. Repeat to make as many bowls as you need. Use them as soon as you can, or store them in a cool, dry atmosphere – moisture in the air will encourage them to go sticky and start to sag.

Canada

Canadian cuisine was shaped by settlers from Britain and France and reflects a heritage of game hunting and fishing which dates back to the original indigenous inhabitants as well as to the intrepid incomers. Bannock, a pan-fried bread, is considered something of a national dish, but was originally brought to the continent by Scottish fur traders. The foodstuff most commonly associated with Canada today is maple syrup – written records do not go far back enough to show when the practice of tapping maple trees for their sweet sap started but Canada has always been the world's biggest producer of maple syrup.

Modern Canadian cuisine reflects the influence of settlers from all over Europe, and in some regions culinary traditions brought in by religious groups who originally came to Canada to avoid persecution at home (such as the Mennonites and Russian Doukhobors) are still in evidence. A strong Jewish community in Montreal plays a part in the cuisine of the area while Quebec retains a strong French style in its food. With a relatively small population in proportion to the size of the country, vast tracts of land are given over to agriculture. Canada is one of the largest agricultural producers and exporters in the world, and many of the Canadians who do not live in the cities are engaged in farming in semi-rural areas.

Barbi Lazarus of the very active Toronto Vegetarian Association (http://veg.ca) put us in touch with Amy Symington, a Canadian vegan chef. Amy writes:

> *I grew up on a small farm in rural southwestern Ontario. We rarely ate packaged food, and if you wanted jam, jelly, pickles, chili sauce, apple sauce, salsa, peaches or pretty much anything that could be jarred, you headed to the cellar, where my mother stored her preserves. My small-but-mighty grandma lived across the road and cultivated a wonderful vegetable garden. We knew where our food came from, or at least most of it.*

It wasn't until I went to university that I began to wonder where the food that Grandma didn't grow came from. After meeting my now husband, a lifelong vegetarian, I began to really look at what good, clean and compassionate eating meant to me and when I turned vegetarian, I found my direction. Not a year later I signed up for culinary school. Now, as a plant-based chef, I have taken all of the tradition and family values I absorbed growing up in rural Canada and I focus on homegrown, well-loved seasonal food and good-quality homemade meals, with a compassionate twist.

Vegetarians and vegans are more likely to run into criticism in the smaller towns – there are more options available in the larger cities. Reactions to vegetarianism vary significantly across the country, as does the general diet. Quebecers love their cheese, the beef farmers in the prairies are partial to steak, East-coasters wouldn't live without lobster, Northerners enjoy the hunt of fishing and West-coasters have a varied, urban yet hippyish style of diet. Ontario is similar to the West coast, eclectic in nature but perhaps there is more of a focus on farm-to-table type food. If you're looking for the best places to live in Canada if you're vegetarian or vegan, Vancouver and Toronto win hands down, in my own opinion. This is not to say that there isn't absolutely amazing vegetarian fare to be found all over the country (there is!); these are just the cities that I believe have the most selection in terms of plant-based restaurants.

The following recipes were devised by Amy Symington.
Amy's website is **ameliaeats.com**

Black bean and chipotle chowder

This thick soup has a rich, hot, smoky flavor that comes from powdered chipotle chilis and cocoa. It can be served over cooked grains (such as quinoa or brown rice) for a filling main course.

Ingredients

1 tsp vegetable oil

4 sticks of celery, diced

3 small carrots, diced

2 small onions, diced

3 cloves of garlic, crushed

1 jalapeno pepper, seeded and finely chopped

1 tbsp cocoa powder

1 tbsp ground chipotle powder

1 tsp cumin

3 medium sweet potatoes, diced

1 lb / 450 g fresh tomatoes, diced

2 pints / 1 litre vegetable stock

2 lb / 900 g canned black beans, drained and rinsed

Zest and juice of 1 lime

1 tsp salt

Fresh cilantro/coriander to garnish

Method

Warm the oil in a large pan and gently fry the onion, carrots and celery for 5 minutes. Stir in the garlic, jalapeno, cocoa, chipotle and cumin and cook until fragrant, about 3 minutes. Add the sweet potatoes, stir together well and cook for a further 3 minutes. Add the tomatoes and stock, bring to the boil, then reduce the heat and simmer, covered, for 25 minutes until the sweet potatoes are tender. Add the beans, lime zest and juice and heat through. Taste and season to taste with salt. Garnish with fresh cilantro/coriander.

CANADA

Veggie poutine

Poutine is a French Canadian culinary innovation. Developed as fast food in 1950s Quebec, it consists of a pile of French fries, topped with fresh curd cheese and smothered in a thin meat gravy. There are various stories about how it was invented – Fernand Lachance of Warwick, Quebec, claims that he is responsible for the name after exclaiming '*ça va faire une maudite poutine*' ('that will make a real mess'). These days, variations are sold everywhere, from greasy spoon diners and chip wagons to the international burger chains, and the dish might contain all kinds of fish, seafood, meat and game. This is a vegan version.

Ingredients

5 potatoes (or sweet potatoes), cut into fries

¼ cup / 60 ml vegetable oil (divided)

Salt and pepper to taste

½ pound / 225 g mixed mushrooms (shiitake, oyster, cremini), wiped and sliced

2 onions, sliced

½ pound / 225 g kale, shredded

⅔ cup / 70 g plain flour

3 pints / 1¼ litres vegetable stock

2 tbsp soy sauce

4 cloves garlic, crushed

2 tomatoes, diced

A handful of fresh chopped herbs (try dill, parsley and thyme)

Method

Preheat the oven to 400°F/200°C. Put the chopped potatoes into a large bowl and toss with 2 tbsp of the oil and salt and pepper. Line two large baking trays with parchment. Divide the fries between the two trays and spread them out. Bake until crispy and golden, about 30 minutes.

Heat 1 tbsp of oil in a large frying pan and gently fry the onion and mushrooms until golden brown. Mix in the shredded kale, heat through and set aside.

Warm the flour in a large saucepan, stirring over a medium heat for 2-3 minutes to toast and bring out the flavor. Slowly whisk in the remaining oil, then whisk in the stock, soy sauce and garlic. Continue to whisk until the gravy is as thick as you like it. Season to taste with salt and pepper and half the fresh herbs.

To serve, put the fries onto a serving platter, top with the reheated mushrooms, onions and kale, ladle gravy on top and finish with the chopped tomatoes and remaining fresh herbs.

CANADA

Apple and fennel salad with orange ginger cider vinaigrette

Ingredients

3 oz / 90 g rocket

1 bulb fennel, julienned (save leaves for garnish)

1 medium green apple, julienned

For the dressing:

2 tbsp apple cider

1 tbsp rapeseed oil

2 tsp maple syrup

1 tsp fresh grated ginger

1 clove garlic, crushed (optional)

1 orange, zested and juiced

Pinch of salt

For the garnish:

$^1/_3$ cup / 50 g toasted walnuts (optional)

Fennel leaves

Method

Make the dressing by whisking all the ingredients together. Put all the salad ingredients into a large serving bowl, toss through the dressing and top with toasted walnuts and fennel leaves.

Ginger maple baked aduki beans

This chapter would not be complete without a dash of maple syrup! This recipe also calls for Worcester sauce – most brands contain anchovies so check the label carefully.

Ingredients

1 tsp rapeseed oil

1 small onion, diced

4 cloves garlic, crushed

2 tbsp fresh grated ginger

1 pound 12 oz / 800 g canned aduki beans, rinsed and drained

5 tbsp tomato paste/purée

5 tbsp maple syrup

1 tbsp vegetarian-friendly Worcester sauce

1 cup / 240 ml water

1½ tsp paprika

¼ tsp cayenne (optional)

2 tsp fresh lemon juice

½ tsp coarse sea salt

Black pepper to taste

Garnish:
Garlic chive micro-greens (optional)

Method

Warm the oil in a large saucepan over a medium heat and gently fry the onions for a minute. Add the garlic and ginger, and sauté until fragrant, about 1 minute. Add the beans, tomato paste/purée, half the maple syrup, Worcester sauce, water, paprika, and cayenne, if using. Stir well, cover and simmer for 20 minutes, stirring occasionally. Next, add the lemon juice, the remaining maple syrup, sea salt and black pepper to taste. Garnish and serve hot.

Orange, rhubarb and ginger crisp

Ingredients

1 lb / 450 g rhubarb, trimmed and cut into $\frac{3}{8}$-inch / 1-cm pieces

2 tsp orange zest

1 tbsp grated ginger

¼ cup / 50 g brown sugar

½ tsp ground cinnamon

For the topping:

¾ cup / 75 g plain wholewheat flour

1¼ cups / 100 g rolled oats

3 tbsp maple syrup

2 tbsp vegetable oil

Method

Preheat the oven to 375°F/190°C. In a large bowl, toss the rhubarb, orange zest, ginger, brown sugar and cinnamon. Transfer to a lightly greased 8 x 8 inch / 20 x 20 cm baking pan. To make the topping, toss together the oats, flour and maple syrup, and gradually mix in the oil with a fork. Sprinkle the topping onto the rhubarb and bake until golden brown, about 45 minutes.

Amy recommends serving this with dairy-free vanilla ice cream and orange slices.

Chile

The archives of the International Vegetarian Union indicate that Chile had its own Vegetarian Society back in the late 19th century. Founded in 1889, the Valparaiso Vegetarian Society boasted a library and reading room, and plans for a restaurant – but just 12 members. Three years later, another mention of it appears, now with 25 members, 'mostly Germans'. This is not as odd as it seems – in the mid-1800s the Chilean government targeted Germany with offers of land and subsidies in order to attract useful, skilled immigrants and in the decades that followed some 40,000 Germans arrived to help colonize the cold and rainy south of the country and improve the economy.

It seems likely that German immigrants brought this small glimmer of vegetarianism with them to Chile, as the typical national diet is very heavily reliant on seafood – in a long, narrow country with a 2,650-mile / 4,240-km coastline, that's hardly surprising. The Chileans devour a vast range of seafood, including razor clams, barnacles and sea urchins.

Maize (*choclo*) was a staple food for the Incas, and is still widely consumed today, although the crop is a little different from the ubiquitous North American sweetcorn, with larger, tougher kernels and a taste that is not so sweet. Quinoa, which is thought to have originated in Peru around 6,000 years ago, is another useful crop in the country.

MENU
Dobladitas
(Chilean breads)
•
Huevos con pilco
de choclo (baked eggs
in corn sauce)
•
Pebre chili dip
•
Milcaos (potato cakes)
•
Calzones rotos (cookies)

The Spanish arrived in Chile in 1541, bringing wheat, rice, citrus fruits and much more, and the combination of Spanish cuisine with native Chilean cuisine is still evident in traditional dishes such as *empanadas* (little pastries generally filled with minced beef), *tortillas* (the Spanish omelet, not the crispy corn snack), *tomatican* (a corn and tomato stew) and *humitas* (a cornmeal paste cooked in corn husks).

Today, a lot of the fresh fruit and vegetables consumed in the country are imported and fresh produce can be a little hard to come by – farmers' markets are a good place to find the freshest fruit and vegetables. Restaurants do not tend to serve vegetable side-dishes, although salads are standard fare. The main meal of the day is eaten at lunchtime, but a wave of British immigrants who arrived between 1880 and 1900 left a legacy of 'teatime' and *té con leche* (tea with milk) is still offered to guests in many homes.

CHILE

Dobladitas (Chilean breads)

Ingredients

6 cups / 600 g plain white flour

½ cup / 120 ml milk

1 tsp salt

1½ cups / 220 g butter, melted, plus 4 tbsp butter, melted, for brushing

2 tsp baking powder

Method

Preheat the oven to 450°F/230°C, and cover a baking tray with baking parchment.

Mix the flour, salt and baking powder together in a large bowl. Stir in the milk and the melted butter (remember to reserve four tablespoons for the next step). Use your hands to mix the wet and dry ingredients together to make a dough, then turn it out onto a floured surface and knead it, adding more flour if necessary, until it is smooth and firm.

Roll the dough out to a thickness of around ¼ inch / ½ cm. Cut circles around 8 inches / 20 cm in diameter – cutting around a small plate can be a good idea. Brush each circle of dough with melted butter and fold in half. Then brush the folded dough with more butter and fold again. Press the folded dough together firmly to seal the layers. Transfer to the prepared baking sheet and bake for 15 minutes until golden brown.

CHILE

Huevos con pilco de choclo (baked eggs in corn sauce)

Ingredients

1 tbsp butter

1 onion

1 lb / 450 g fresh or frozen sweetcorn kernels

1½ cups / 360 ml milk

Salt and black pepper, to taste

2 tbsp chopped fresh basil

4 eggs

Method

Preheat the oven to 400°F/200°C. Grease one large shallow oven-proof dish or four individual-sized dishes.

Peel the onion and chop it finely. In a saucepan, fry it gently in the butter until soft and translucent. Stir in the sweetcorn and milk, bring to boiling point, then reduce the heat to a simmer and cook, stirring frequently, until the mixture is quite thick. Stir in the basil and season with salt and pepper, then spoon the warm mixture into the oven dish(es). Smooth the top of the mixture and make an indentation to hold each egg. Carefully crack the eggs into the indentations – it's safest to crack each egg individually into a jug and then pour it into the indentation in the corn mixture. Top with a few extra dots of butter and an extra twist of black pepper.

Bake for 8-10 minutes, so that the egg white sets and turns opaque, and the egg yolk is set but soft. Serve immediately with warm dobladitas.

CHILE

Pebre chili dip

This popular condiment is widely used in sandwiches or as a dip. It's as hot as you choose to make it... and beware, it's hotter the day after it is made!

Ingredients

1 onion

3 cloves garlic

2-3 tbsp finely chopped fresh red or green chilis

1-2 tbsp red wine

1-2 tbsp olive oil

Juice of ½ lime

A handful of fresh chopped cilantro/ coriander

Salt and pepper to taste

Method

Peel and finely chop the onion, and peel and crush the garlic. Stir all the ingredients together in a large bowl, adding the lime juice and seasoning according to your own taste. Pebre can be stored in a jar in the refrigerator for a week.

Milcaos (potato cakes)

These traditional potato cakes are made with a mixture of mashed and raw, grated potato which makes for a lighter texture than using dense mashed potato alone. In Chile they would normally be made with lard – I substituted vegetable suet, a solid white vegetable fat which comes in little pellets. These are mixed into the potato, and melt away as the mixture is frying, creating crispy holes in the cooked potato cakes.

Ingredients

6 medium potatoes

1 tbsp butter (or vegan margarine)

2 tbsp vegetable suet

Vegetable oil for frying

Salt to taste

Method

Peel the potatoes and boil half of them in salted water until tender. Drain and mash with the butter or vegan margarine. Grate the remaining potatoes finely, wrap them in a clean, dry dishcloth and squeeze firmly to dry the potato as much as you can.

Put the mashed potato, raw grated potato, vegetable suet and salt into a large bowl and mix them together well – using your hands is the best way. Keep squeezing and kneading in the bowl until the mixture comes together as a smooth dough. Shape the dough into flat, circular patties around 3 inches / 8 cm in diameter.

Fill a wok or deep frying pan with vegetable oil to a depth of around 2 inches / 5 cm. Bring the oil to frying temperature (test by dropping a little of the dough in – it should sizzle rather than sink) and fry the potato cakes in small batches, turning carefully until they are golden and crispy. Drain on paper towels before serving with hot pepper sauce.

Calzones rotos (cookies)

Calzones rotos translates as 'torn underwear' – the name probably reflects the unusual twisted shape of these traditional fried cookies, although there is a folk tale which claims they are named after an unfortunate street-seller, whose torn underwear was revealed when a gust of wind blew her skirt up while she was selling them in the marketplace. They're fun to make, but can be tricky at first – make your dough firm, don't roll it too thinly and don't try to make them too tiny – you'll soon get the hang of it!

Ingredients

2¼ cups / 225 g plain white flour

½ cup / 60 g icing sugar,
  plus extra for dusting

1 tsp salt

1½ tsp baking powder

2 whole eggs plus 1 egg yolk

Zest of half a lemon

3 tbsp butter, softened

2 tbsp brandy (use traditional
  Chilean Pisco if you can!)

Vegetable oil for frying

Method

Put the flour, icing sugar, salt and baking power in a large mixing bowl and stir together well. In a separate small bowl, beat the eggs and egg yolk with the lemon zest. Stir the wet ingredients into the dry ingredients, then add the softened butter and use your hands to mix everything together. Add the brandy, a little at a time, kneading between each addition until your dough is smooth, firm and pliable. Wrap it in plastic wrap and chill for 20 minutes.

Prepare a floured surface. Roll the dough out to a thickness of around ¼ inch / ½ cm. Use a sharp knife to cut the rolled dough into strips about 2 inches / 5 cm wide. Then divide each strip into rectangles about 4 inches / 10 cm long.

Now for the tricky bit: using a sharp knife, make a cut 1 inch / 2.5 cm long, lengthways, in the middle of one of the pieces of dough. Carefully pull one end of the dough through this hole to make a shape a bit like a bow. Use the dough to make as many cookies as you can – it's fine to re-roll the trimmings.

Fill a wok or deep frying pan with vegetable oil to a depth of around 2 inches / 5 cm. Heat the oil to frying temperature and fry the cookies in small batches, turning occasionally, until they are golden and crisp. Carefully lift them out of the oil, let them drain on kitchen paper and then dust liberally with icing sugar.

China

At first glance, Chinese cuisine seems to be one of the best-known international styles of cookery, with Chinese migrants creating successful restaurants all over the world. But China is a vast country, and the concept of 'Chinese' food is a massive over-generalization.

The style most recognizable to Western diners is Cantonese food, which tends to use soy sauce, black bean sauce, oyster sauce and hoisin sauce as its principal flavorings. The best Cantonese food is fantastically fresh, with crisp, colorful stir-fries using very little oil.

Sichuan food is more fiery, with chilis and hot peppercorns frequently used, alongside more subtle garlic and ginger. Fujian food is famed for its use of edible fungi and bamboo shoots. Northern (Beijing-style) food, unlike that of other areas, tends to use grains, corn and soybeans as its staples, with wheat-based noodles and steamed buns served more often than rice, and is considered to be an ancient and venerable cookery style developed to please China's exacting Emperors.

Overall, Chinese food tends to be relatively vegetarian- and vegan-friendly. Although fish and sea-food are widely enjoyed, dairy foods are not a big part of the diet, and of course China is the original home of tofu and tempeh, fantastic protein sources for vegetarians and vegans. Chinese Buddhism advocates vegetarianism and as a consequence, vegetarian food has been in a continuous state of development in China for centuries.

MENU

Sweet and sour tofu
with vegetables

•

Longevity noodles

•

ABC soup

•

Chinese greens

•

Sweet potato and
ginger dessert

It's almost possible to draw a line on a map, to divide the Asian cultures that rely heavily on dairy foods, such as India and Tibet, from those that tend to reject dairy foods. Early Chinese dynasties enjoyed goats' milk and fermented mares' milk, but the land and climate were more suitable for rice paddies than grazing cattle. Using soya products meant more people could be fed economically, but there may also be a cultural reluctance to drink milk because it was once associated with nomadic borderland tribes.

Traditionally, Chinese meals aim to provide a balance of Yin (cooling) and Yang (warming) foods. Clear soups and fruits and vegetables are Yin; meat and starchy foods are Yang. With small portions of fresh, colorful vegetables, thoughtfully chopped into attractive shapes, Chinese food can be a work of art. At a shared meal, each diner is given an individual bowl of rice, but the remaining dishes are presented in larger, communal portions. Each diner uses chopsticks to pick food out of the communal dishes, bite by bite.

These recipes were contributed by Mohana Gill (see pages 192-3).

CHINA

Sweet and sour tofu with vegetables

A favorite and now classic flavor combination, modern sweet and sour sauces have roots in China but are often influenced by Western tastes. This easy sauce works beautifully with tofu and crisp green peppers. Serve with a dish of steaming white rice.

Ingredients

1 tbsp cornflour

¾ cup / 180 ml vegetable stock

3 tbsp sugar

3 tbsp white wine vinegar

1 tbsp tomato ketchup

2 tbsp soy sauce

½ tsp ground ginger

¼ tsp cayenne pepper

2 cloves garlic, finely chopped

1 onion

2 carrots

1 green bell pepper

A few mushrooms

14 oz / 400 g firm tofu

2 tbsp vegetable oil

Method

To make the sauce, first mix the cornflour into the vegetable stock, then add the sugar, vinegar, ketchup, soy sauce, ginger and cayenne and mix well.

Peel the onions, carrot and garlic. Chop the onions finely, crush the garlic and slice the carrot. Trim and slice the mushrooms. Deseed and dice the green bell pepper. Drain the tofu, press gently in kitchen paper to remove excess water and then cut into 1-inch / 2.5-cm cubes.

Heat the oil in a wok and stir-fry the onion, garlic and carrots for about 5 minutes. Add the pepper and mushrooms and cook for a further 2 minutes. Then pour in the sauce and cook until the mixture thickens and looks glossy. Finally, gently stir in the tofu and let the dish bubble gently for 5 minutes before serving hot.

CHINA

Longevity noodles

Longevity noodles symbolize long life and are a popular dish to serve at birthdays or Chinese New Year celebrations.

There's a saying in China that translates as: 'Firewood, rice, oil, salt, soy sauce, vinegar and tea are the seven daily necessities.' Chinese vinegar comes in three varieties – white, black and red. The white version has the taste closest to Western wine vinegars; the black version is rich and smoky, and can serve as an alternative to balsamic vinegar. The red vinegar used in this recipe has a distinctive sweet-tart flavor. If you can't find it, red wine vinegar with a dash of sugar or honey will do the job.

Oyster sauce is a nuisance for vegetarians dining in Chinese restaurants as it is used in many dishes, but there is a vegetarian brand available and if you cook Chinese food regularly, it's well worth seeking it out, rather than omitting the oyster sauce altogether.

Ingredients

1 pack dried thin noodles

1 tbsp Chinese red vinegar

1 tsp sesame oil

1½ tsp light soy sauce

1 tbsp vegetarian oyster sauce

1 tsp cornflour

3 scallions/spring onions, sliced

A handful of chopped garlic chives

1 inch / 2.5 cm fresh ginger root

2 cloves garlic

20 fresh shiitake mushrooms

¼ cup / 60 ml vegetable oil

1 cup / 240 ml warm water

Method

Cook the noodles in boiling water until tender, then drain and set aside.
In a small bowl, mix the vinegar, sesame oil, soy sauce, vegetarian oyster sauce and cornflour.

Trim and chop the scallions/spring onions and garlic chives. Peel the ginger and garlic, and slice them thinly. Remove the woody stalks from the shiitake mushrooms – discard them or reserve them to make a flavorful stock. Wipe and slice the mushroom caps.

Heat the oil in a wok and stir-fry the ginger and garlic for 30 seconds. Add the mushrooms, spring onions and garlic chives. Stir-fry for 30 seconds, then add the sauce, mix thoroughly, and add a cup of warm water. Let the mixture bubble for about 2 minutes, then stir in the noodles, toss and heat through before serving.

ABC soup

Commonly served in Chinese homes as part of a meal, this clear soup is surprisingly delicious and easy to prepare. The key to the authentic flavor is white pepper, a spice that has fallen out of favor in the West where 'freshly ground black pepper' seems to appear on the end of every recipe's list of ingredients!

Ingredients

1 large potato

1 medium carrot

1 onion

1 large tomato

3-4 white peppercorns, crushed or ground

2 cups / 500 ml vegetable stock

Salt and pepper to taste

Method

Peel the vegetables and chop them all into bite-sized pieces. Bring the stock to boiling point in a large pan. Add the vegetables and simmer for 20-30 minutes until soft. Add the white pepper and adjust the seasoning to suit your taste. Serve hot.

Chinese greens

No Chinese meal is complete without a dish of fresh greens.

Ingredients

2 bunches long-stem broccoli

¼ cup / 60 ml vegetarian oyster sauce

1 clove garlic, crushed

1½ tbsp light soy sauce

1 tsp sugar

1 tbsp vegetable oil

1 tsp sesame oil

Method

Mix the vegetarian oyster sauce, garlic, soy sauce and sugar together – shaking them in a small jar is an easy way to do this.

Trim the broccoli and slice any thick stems lengthways. Plunge into a large pan of boiling salted water and cook for 3 minutes, then drain and refresh under cold running water – this halts the cooking process and keeps the vegetables crisp and bright green. Arrange the broccoli on a serving plate.

Warm the vegetable and sesame oil together over a high heat for 30 seconds, then pour over the broccoli and drizzle the sauce on top.

CHINA

Sweet potato and ginger dessert

Desserts are not always served with Chinese meals and some Chinese restaurants do not offer any 'puddings', much to the disappointment of Western customers. Basic fruit-based sweet dishes may be served as part of the main meal. Sweet snacks are popular, often fried morsels incorporating red bean paste. If dessert is served at the end of the meal, it is usually sliced fresh fruit, or a sweet soup made with red beans and sugar.

This recipe is, however, a traditional favorite, revered for its heartwarming and revitalizing properties. Find the dried dates in Chinese groceries – they have a distinctive flavor.

Ingredients

2 sweet potatoes

2 inches / 5 cm fresh ginger root

3½ cups / 840 ml water

8 dried red dates

⅓ cup / 60 g brown sugar

Method

Peel the sweet potatoes and chop into chunks. Peel and slice the ginger. Bring the water to the boil, then add the sweet potatoes, ginger and dates, and simmer for 15 minutes. Add the sugar, increase the heat to bring the mixture to boiling point and boil until the sugar has dissolved and the sweet potatoes are cooked through.

This dessert can be served hot or cold. Mohana says that it is a great remedy for a winter cold!

Cuba

Cuban food is not typically Caribbean, and reflects a variety of influences. The indigenous people cultivated black beans, cassava, yams and maize, but there is little trace left of their traditional cuisine as most of the population was wiped out, either by massacre or disease, after Columbus claimed the island for Spain in 1492. The Spanish brought new crops and a different (*criollo*) style of eating.

Later, the Spanish began to import African slaves and there is some evidence that, although they were not able to bring any African foods with them, they retained their own style of cooking, which has had a lasting influence on Cuban food. The mid-19th century saw an influx of Chinese workers gradually spread a taste for Chinese food around the island – in Havana, a mixture of olives, capers and raisins (*alcaparrado*) creates a popular sweet and sour flavor that crops up in a variety of dishes. Modern Cuban cookery is also influenced by the flavors of the Caribbean, North America and Mexico.

After the Cuban Revolution of 1959, many wealthy people, including restaurant owners, fled the country. Food shortages became frequent and trade restrictions imposed on Cuba because of political differences have led to rationing and poor-quality food. In spite of rationing, or perhaps because of it, meat (generally pork and chicken, and some beef) is eagerly consumed. Vegetarian and vegan visitors report that it is very difficult to find genuine vegetarian food (rather than meat stew with the meat chunks scooped out!). Omelets are the order of the day, and even a cheese sandwich is off limits because the traditional long Cuban breads are made with lard. Vegans are likely to struggle,

MENU

Moros y Cristianos (black beans and rice)

•

Cuban salad

•

Chichachirritas (plantain fritters) with mojo

•

Torrejas (Cuban-style French toast)

although there are a handful of pioneering vegetarian restaurants in Havana.

Most restaurants are government owned, with a reputation for bland food and indifferent service. Some people operate small restaurants from their own homes, called *paladares* – these are subject to some government restrictions that affect the number of people and the type of food that can be served, but the home-cooked food is still generally likely to be better than that offered by the government-owned eateries, and the proprietors are likely to be a little more flexible and open to meat-free suggestions!

Leaving aside the prevalence of meat, the three key constituents of Cuban food are bean soups and stews, rice and fried root vegetables. The bean soups probably came from Spain and may be thick or thin, made with black beans, white beans, kidney beans or garbanzos/chickpeas. Cuban food is not highly spiced, and soups and stews are generally flavored with a *sofrito* – a fried mixture of finely chopped onions, garlic, green bell pepper, tomatoes and herbs, typically oregano, bay leaves and cumin.

Desserts are very sweet and typically include ice cream, baked custards and fruit such as guava, papaya, mango, citrus fruits and grated coconut poached in a sticky sugar syrup. It has been suggested that the Cuban sweet tooth dates back to the days when a large population of slaves in the country supplemented their meager diet by chewing on the sugar cane that they tended.

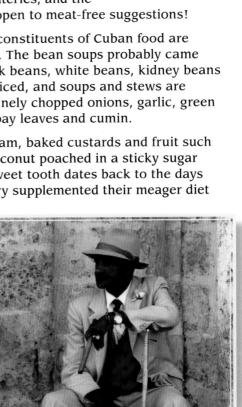

Moros y Cristianos (Black beans and rice)

Ingredient

1 lb 12 oz / 800 g canned black beans

1 large onion, diced

3 garlic cloves, crushed

1 green bell pepper, deseeded and chopped

Olive oil, for frying

3 tbsp tomato paste/purée

3 tsp ground cumin

1¼ cups / 200 g long grain white rice

2 cups / 500 ml vegetable stock

Salt and pepper, to taste

Method

Drain and rinse the beans.

In a large pan with a lid, fry the onion, garlic and green bell pepper in the olive oil until tender. Add the tomato paste, black beans, cumin, rice and stock.

Cover the pan and cook over a low heat for about 30 minutes until the rice is cooked. Season to taste.

Cuban salad

Ingredients

1 head of crisp lettuce

2 ripe tomatoes

2 radishes, very thinly sliced

1 onion, very thinly sliced

For the dressing:

½ cup / 120 ml olive oil

2 tbsp white vinegar

2 tbsp lemon juice

2 cloves garlic, crushed

Salt and black pepper to taste

Method

Separate the lettuce into leaves, and rinse and dry them if necessary. Cut the tomatoes into wedges. Mix all the salad vegetables together in a large serving bowl.

Mix all the dressing ingredients together. Just before serving, pour the dressing over the salad, a little at a time, tossing the vegetables until they are well covered.

CUBA

Chichachirritas (plantain fritters) with mojo

Traditionally served with both meat and vegetables, the Cuban mojo sauce has its roots in the Canary Islands, from where many immigrants have come to Cuba. In Cuba, it is made with the juice from sour oranges. This recipe uses the more widely available sweet orange juice combined with lime juice to add acidity.

Ingredients

2 green plantains

vegetable oil for deep frying

Salt or garlic salt

For the mojo:

⅓ cup / 80 ml olive oil

6 cloves of garlic, crushed

Juice of 1 large orange

Juice of 2 limes

½ tsp ground cumin

Salt and pepper to taste

Method

First make the mojo. Warm the olive oil in a deep pan and sauté the garlic for just about 30 seconds. Add the orange and lime juice, cumin and seasoning. Be prepared for the sauce to spit! Bring the mixture to a rolling boil, boil for 3 minutes and then leave to cool. Mojo is best used on the day it is made, but can be stored in a jar in the fridge for a few days.

Peel the plantains and slice them into rounds as thin as you can make them – use a mandolin if you have one. Heat the oil in a deep fat fryer, wok or deep heavy frying pan, and deep fry the plantain slices in small batches, taking care that they do not clump together. Drain on kitchen towels, sprinkle with salt or garlic salt and mojo, and serve immediately.

CUBA

Torrejas (Cuban-style French toast)

This Cuban-style French toast is an everyday favorite.

Ingredients

8 slices of bread

4 eggs

1 can evaporated milk

2 tbsp white cooking wine

1 cup / 200 g sugar

1 tsp vanilla extract

1 tsp ground cinnamon

Oil for shallow frying

Syrup or jam

Method

Beat the eggs together with the milk, wine, sugar, vanilla and cinnamon. Heat the oil in a frying pan. Dip the bread into the wet mixture and fry on both sides until golden brown. Drizzle with warmed jam or syrup to serve.

Denmark

Sune Borkfelt from the Danish Vegetarian Society (**vegetarforening.dk**) introduced me to Kirsten Skaarup, who has written more than 20 vegetarian cookbooks in Danish. Asked if she could share some examples of typical Danish vegetarian dishes, she was blunt: 'I can give you some recipes, but they will not be typically Danish. We are the most meat-eating country in the world and have no history in this field.'

There are probably more than a few countries that would lay claim to being the 'most meat-eating' in the world. But if you ask somebody to name a food synonymous with Denmark, the answer is likely to be 'bacon'. Denmark currently exports more than 2 million tonnes of pork per year and some vegetarian travelers have reported that, because of the ubiquitous and enormously popular sausage stands, the whole country seems to smell of cooking sausages!

But meat wasn't always as abundantly available in Denmark. Dairy farming was dominant, so cattle were not bred for meat, or slaughtered early. By the time their 'productive' lives were deemed to be at an end, the meat they yielded was not particularly appetizing. *Frikadeller*, Danish meatballs, widely considered to be the national dish, were surely invented as a way to make the best of the scraps of meat available. Fish also plays a prominent role in Danish cuisine, with pickled herring and smoked fish perennially popular. The Danish word for meat is *kød*, which is perhaps indicative of the major role played by fish in the early Danish diet.

Rye bread forms the base of the classic Danish open sandwich (*smorrebrod*) – it hasn't changed much since it was mentioned in the Viking sagas. In medieval times it was generally spread with butter or lard, and in the 16th century slices of bread were commonly used instead of plates. These days, there are

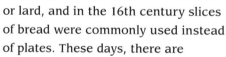

hundreds of varieties of open sandwiches on offer, and almost without exception they are decked with fish, sausage, cold meat slices and meat paté.

The Danish government has taken tough action to improve the nation's health, but a tax on foods high in saturated fats was recently scrapped because it only increased the price of food and sent people over the border to Germany to do their shopping. Denmark has made an impression at the high end of gastronomy in recent years, however, with Nordic cuisine attracting interest from gourmands and a handful of Danish restaurants winning Michelin stars for their innovative use of fresh, seasonal, traditional produce.

Vegetarian visitors attracted by tales of the new Nordic gastronomy may be frustrated when looking for food in Danish restaurants, as even dishes based primarily on potatoes or other vegetables, and salads, are very likely to contain bits of bacon or ham. The sensible thing to do is probably to avoid traditional Danish food altogether and look for sustenance at curry houses, and, although it seems counter-intuitive, the popular Turkish kebab shops, where you should find falafels, tabbouleh and salad-filled pitas.

Kirsten's vegetarian inventions draw on Danish traditions – a first course of soup, followed by a buffet-style offering of crunchy almond rissoles (the vegetarian answer to frikadeller!), baked beetroot with horseradish and tasty stuffed cabbage leaves. Her blog is **atkodfrifredag.dk** ('meat-free Friday').

MENU

Jerusalem artichoke soup

•

Baked beetroot

•

Almond rissoles

•

Cabbage rolls

•

Aeblekage (apple charlotte)

DENMARK

Jerusalem artichoke soup

Ingredients

1 oz / 30 g shallots

4 cloves garlic

2 tbsp olive oil

10 oz / 300 g Jerusalem artichokes

7 oz / 200 g potatoes

4 oz / 125 g carrots

2 tsp dried thyme

1 pint / 2 litres vegetable stock

Lemon juice, to taste

3 tbsp hazelnuts

A sprig of fresh thyme

Method

Peel and finely chop the shallots and garlic. Sauté them gently in the oil until golden. Peel the artichokes, then select a small one and slice it thinly – this will be used to garnish the soup later. Chop the rest of the artichokes into small pieces. Peel and chop the potatoes and carrots. Add them to the shallots along with the vegetable stock and dried thyme.

Bring the soup to the boil and let it bubble for 10 minutes, until all the vegetables are tender. Allow it to cool a little, then transfer to a blender and purée until smooth.

Chop the hazelnuts coarsely and dry-roast them in a heavy-bottomed pan until they begin to color. Set them aside. Fry the reserved artichoke slices in a little oil until they are golden and crisp, then transfer to a sheet of kitchen towel to drain. Reheat the soup and season to taste with a little lemon juice. Serve each portion garnished with a few of the toasted hazelnut pieces, the artichoke crisps and a few fresh thyme leaves.

DENMARK

Baked beetroot

Ingredients

4 medium beetroots

6 tbsp mayonnaise

fresh grated horseradish, to taste

Cress, to garnish

Method

Preheat the oven to 300°F/150°C. Scrub the beetroots well – leave the root and some of the leaves intact. This stops them from 'bleeding' and makes for a lovely presentation – and the whole thing is edible. Transfer them to a baking tray and bake them for 40-50 minutes, depending on their size.

Mix the mayonnaise with a little grated horseradish – the amount you choose to add is up to you! Serve the roasted beetroots sliced into quarters with the mayonnaise, cress and some toasted rye bread.

Almond rissoles

Ingredients

¼ cup / 50 g red lentils

2 oz / 50 g shallots

3 cloves garlic

2 oz / 50 g red bell pepper

4 oz / 100 g carrots

1 cup / 100 g almonds

⅔ cup / 50 g rolled oats

2 tbsp soy sauce

2 tbsp plain flour

A handful of chopped parsley

2 eggs

Olive oil, for frying

Salt and pepper, to taste

Method

Put the lentils into a saucepan, cover them with water and simmer for 20 minutes. Drain well and set aside.

Chop the shallots, garlic and red bell pepper finely. Grate the carrot finely. Chop the almonds quite finely – you aren't aiming to reduce them to a powder, but they shouldn't be too chunky. Mix the almonds with the vegetables, lentils, oats and soy sauce, and season with salt and pepper. Mix the flour with two tablespoons of water and stir into the mixture. Add the parsley and beaten eggs.

Let the mixture stand for half an hour, then see if the consistency will allow you to shape it into small 'meatballs'. If it's too sticky to handle, add more oats. Shape the mixture into approximately 12 little patties and shallow fry them gently until crisp and golden.

Cabbage rolls with sour/sweet filling and mustard sauce

I love Kirsten's tasty filling for this dish – adding tofu to the mixture gives it the protein component that, for me, elevates these stuffed cabbage rolls from a vegetable side dish to a main dish.

Ingredients

½ cup / 100 g red lentils

5 oz / 150 g leeks

2 oz / 50 g shallots

4 cloves garlic

2 tbsp olive oil

5 oz / 150 g apples

½ cup / 50 g peanuts

⅓ cup / 50 g raisins

4 tsp dried thyme

1 tbsp lemon juice

5 oz / 150 g firm tofu

2 leaves kale or a generous handful of chopped parsley

2-3 tbsp soy sauce

10 large savoy cabbage leaves

for the mustard sauce:

2 cups / 500 ml soya cream

2-3 tbsp mustard

1-2 tbsp soy sauce

Lemon juice

Freshly ground pepper

Method

Put the lentils into a saucepan, cover them with water and simmer them for 20 minutes. Transfer to a sieve and allow to drain.

Trim and finely chop the leeks. Peel and finely chop the shallots and garlic. Sauté the leeks, garlic and shallots in the oil until soft and translucent.

Peel and core the apple, and chop it into small pieces. Roughly chop the nuts and raisins. Add to the leek mixture with the lemon juice and the dried thyme, and continue to cook for a few more minutes.

Drain and crumble the tofu. Chop the parsley or kale finely. Stir these into the filling mixture, season to taste with salt, pepper and soy sauce, and allow to cool.

Blanch the cabbage leaves in a pot of boiling water for a few minutes, until soft and pliable. Drain them and trim away any thick ribs. Place a spoonful of the filling on each leaf, fold in the sides and roll up as tightly as you can. Secure the cabbage rolls with a cocktail stick and arrange them in an ovenproof dish. The rolls can be made ahead to this point, and chilled until you are ready for them.

To cook the rolls, preheat the oven to 480°F/250°C. Brush them with a little oil and bake them for 5 minutes. Then pop the dish under the grill and cook until the cabbage rolls are golden on top.

To make the mustard sauce, mix the soya cream with mustard, soy sauce, freshly ground pepper and a little lemon juice. The sauce can be served hot or cold.

DENMARK

DENMARK

Aeblekage (apple charlotte)

Apples are used in many traditional Danish desserts – they were a home-grown fruit that could be stored and used through the winter months. This dish is a perennial favorite and makes a simple apple purée into something altogether more elegant. Make it your own by adding some raisins, orange zest or chopped dates, a splash of calvados or a splodge of sour cream.

Ingredients

1 lb / 450 g cooking apples

1 lemon

4-5 tbsp honey

½ cup / 75g fresh white breadcrumbs

⅔ cup / 100 g caster sugar

¾ cup / 75 g hazelnuts, chopped

Method

Peel, core and chop the apples. Put them into a large, heavy-bottomed pan. Add the zest and juice of the lemon and cook gently for 10 minutes until the apples begin to break down. Mash them up with a wooden spoon and, while they are still warm, mix in as much honey as you like – some people like their apples quite tart. Set the apple mixture aside to cool – or chill if you want to enjoy the dish really cold.

Put the breadcrumbs into a frying pan and stir in the sugar. Heat the mixture gently, stirring continually, until the sugar melts and the breadcrumbs become crisp and golden – take care not to let the mixture burn. When you judge that it is perfectly crisp and not too brown, tip it onto a plate to stop it from cooking further.

Divide half of the apple mixture between four glass serving dishes. Cover each with a layer of the sweet, crispy crumbs. Divide the rest of the apple mixture between the dishes and finish with the rest of the breadcrumbs and the chopped nuts. Serve immediately, while the crumbs are still crisp!

Egypt

The fact that Egypt has an amazing history as a wealthy and powerful nation is due in part to the river that runs through it. The banks of the Nile have always been wonderfully fertile, and even the earliest civilizations learned to dig ditches to divert some water to irrigate the land nearby. But with land falling into two categories – that which was richly fertile, and the desert – there were few areas that were really suitable for grazing livestock.

For something like 2,000 years, between the closing of the last pagan temple and the arrival of Islam, Egypt was part of the Eastern Roman or Byzantine Empire and the dominant religion was Coptic Orthodox Christianity. This imposed dietary limitations on nearly 200 days of the year, with fish permitted but no other animals or animal products, and a completely vegan diet on nearly 60 days of the year.

The combination of religious dietary dictates, little land for grazing and abundant fresh fruit, vegetables, herbs and spices led the Egyptians to develop a large repertoire of vegetarian and vegan dishes, and modern Egyptian cuisine remains quite vegetarian-friendly. Many of the dishes enjoyed routinely in Egypt are suitable for vegetarians or vegans – dips and salads with

MENU

Shorbet ads
(lentil soup)

•

Kosheri (lentils,
beans and rice)

•

Mahshy (stuffed
eggplant/aubergine)

•

Couscous with currants
and ginger

•

Al burtugal wal zabib al
mutabal (spiced oranges)

pita bread, *tamaya* (the Egyptian equivalent of falafel), *foul* (mashed fava beans), *molokhia* (a slimy green soupy stew made from a plant we know as Jew's Mallow, not unlike spinach), pasta and vegetables.

However, most Egyptians are not familiar with the concept of vegetarianism and, away from the popular tourist resorts, asking for vegetarian food can generate some blank looks. With most main courses likely to contain meat or fish, vegetarians looking for sustenance off the beaten track will probably rely on dips, cooked vegetables and pulses, and breads. Salads, fresh fruit and uncooked vegetables, whether washed or not, can cause stomach problems for the unwary traveler. Kosheri, a mixture of lentils, rice, garbanzos/chickpeas and sometimes pasta, with fried onions and a vinegary tomato sauce, is a filling, vegan-friendly dish that is widely available and served from vans on the streets and in Kosheri restaurants, where the menu often consists of just three choices – small, medium or large!

EGYPT

Shorbet ads (lentil soup)

Simple ingredients create a soup that is tasty, nutritious, satisfying and very cheap!

Ingredients

1½ cups / 225 g red lentils

2½ pints / 1¼ litres vegetable stock

1 large onion, roughly chopped

2 tomatoes, roughly chopped

1 carrot, peeled and roughly chopped

Juice of ½ a lemon

1 tsp ground cumin

Salt and pepper

Method

Put the lentils, stock, onion, tomatoes and carrots into a large saucepan. Bring to the boil, then simmer gently for 30 minutes until the lentils are disintegrating and the vegetables are cooked. Stir from time to time to make sure it doesn't stick to the bottom of the pan, and top up with a little extra water if necessary.

Allow the soup to cool a little and then transfer to a food processor, or use a stick blender, and blend until smooth. Pour it back into the pan and check the consistency – you might like to add more vegetable stock to thin it down. Add the lemon juice, cumin and seasoning. Reheat to serve.

Kosheri (lentils, beans and rice)

Many versions of this dish also include a layer of cooked pasta – if you would like to add some, too, use macaroni or small pasta shapes. The trickiest part of this recipe is timing – you need the rice, lentils, sauce and garbanzos/chickpeas all to be warm when you layer them onto the serving dish. This is traditionally quite a vinegary dish (not unlike British chips!) – add the vinegar slowly and sample as you go to make it right for your own taste.

Ingredients

2 large onions, finely chopped

1 tbsp vegetable oil (for frying)

2 cups / 300 g long-grain white rice

1⅓ cups / 200 g brown lentils

2 tsp olive oil (for sauce)

6-8 cloves of garlic, roughly chopped

18 oz / 500 g passata (sieved tomatoes)

¼ cup / 60 ml vinegar

Cayenne, to taste

Salt, to taste

14 oz / 400 g canned garbanzo beans/chickpeas

Method

Warm the vegetable oil in a frying pan and fry the onions until they are crisp and almost burnt. Scoop them onto a paper towel to drain, but save the cooking oil.

Put the rice into a medium-sized saucepan and cover it with water. Bring to the boil, cover, and simmer on the lowest possible heat, undisturbed, for about 20 minutes, until the rice is tender. Drain the rice and stir in the reserved oniony oil.

Put the lentils into a medium-sized saucepan and cover them with water. Bring to the boil, cover and simmer gently for about 20 minutes, until tender but not disintegrating. Drain and season with salt.

While the lentils and rice are cooking, make the tomato sauce. Heat the olive oil in a medium-sized saucepan and gently fry the garlic for a minute or two – it should be slightly browned but not burnt. Stir in the passata, heat it through and then stir in the vinegar and season according to your taste with cayenne and salt.

Warm the garbanzos/chickpeas through – you can use a microwave if you have one, or tip the contents of the tin into a small pan and heat on the hob. Spread half the rice in a layer on a large serving dish. Top it with a layer of lentils, then the rest of the rice, then the drained chickpeas. Pour the sauce over the top and finish with the crispy fried onions. Serve warm.

EGYPT

Mahshy (stuffed eggplant/aubergine)

Mahshy means 'stuffed' and can be applied to cabbage leaves, vine leaves, potatoes and zucchinis/courgettes as well as eggplants/aubergines. If you can't find baby eggplants/aubergines, use grown-up ones. Halve them lengthways or slice them thickly widthways, scoop out the seeds, fill them with the stuffing, and bake in the same way, slowly, under foil and covered in stock. The cooking time will depend on the size of the eggplants/aubergines. If you do find baby ones, see if you can also find a corer for them – an internet search might be the best way to get hold of one of these handy gadgets!

Ingredients

2 lb 3 oz / 1 kg baby eggplants/aubergines

2 tbsp olive oil

1 onion, chopped

2 lb 3 oz / 1 kg fresh tomatoes, chopped

A handful of fresh chopped parsley

²/₃ cup / 100 g white short-grain rice

Salt and pepper, to taste

2 cups / 500 ml vegetable stock, warm

Method

Preheat the oven to 340°F/170°C.

Wash and core the eggplants/aubergines, and prick the skins with a fork. Heat the oil in a large saucepan and gently cook the onions with the tomatoes and parsley, for 5 minutes. Remove from the heat, stir in the rice, mix together thoroughly and leave to cool for 10 minutes.

Fill the eggplants/aubergines with the rice and arrange them in the base of a deep baking dish. Pour the warm stock over them and cover the dish tightly with foil. Bake until the rice is tender – around 40 minutes.

Couscous with currants and ginger

Ingredients

1¼ cups / 200 g couscous

⅓ cup / 50 g currants

1 onion, finely chopped

2 cloves garlic, crushed

1 tbsp grated root ginger

1 tsp cumin seeds

Grated zest of 1 orange

1 tbsp chopped fresh cilantro/coriander

2 tsp olive oil

Salt and hot chili flakes, to taste

Method

Mix the couscous and currants together in a large bowl. Pour 1 cup / 250 ml of boiling water on top and leave to stand for at least 5 minutes.

Put the cumin seeds into a dry, heavy-bottomed pan and heat them gently until they begin to brown and release their aromatic oils. Stir them frequently to prevent them from burning. As soon as a waft of scent comes off the pan, turn the seeds onto a plate to stop them from cooking further, and leave them to cool.

Warm the oil in a large frying pan and gently fry the onion, garlic and ginger for around 3 minutes, stirring constantly, until the onion is tender and translucent. Add the cumin seeds and cook for another minute.

Fluff up the couscous with a fork and stir in the cooked onions, the orange zest and the fresh cilantro/coriander. Season to suit your taste with salt and hot chili flakes.

EGYPT

Al burtugal wal zabib al mutabal (spiced oranges)

Ingredients

4 large oranges

1 cup / 120 g sugar

$^2/_3$ cup / 80 g sultanas

2 cinnamon sticks

Juice of 1 lemon

½ tsp ground allspice

1 tbsp crystalized ginger, finely chopped

Method

Use a sharp knife to peel the oranges, removing all the white pith if you can. Slice thinly, widthways, and discard any pips. Put the orange slices into a shallow heat-proof bowl.

Put the sugar into a small saucepan with ½ cup / 120 ml water and bring to the boil, stirring to make sure the sugar dissolves. Add the sultanas, cinnamon sticks, ginger, allspice and lemon juice and simmer gently until it begins to thicken and bubble – about 10 minutes.

Pour the hot syrup over the orange slices, making sure that they are all well coated, and then allow to cool. Chill before serving.

England

Vegetarianism has existed all over the world for a very long time, but the English Victorians were the first to decide that vegetarians needed a 'society' to protect their interests and campaign in support of the diet. The Vegetarian Society (vegsoc.org) was born in Salford, in the rather grim industrial northwest of England, in 1847. One could argue that there were no vegetarians before then, since it was the Vegetarian Society that actually invented the word 'vegetarian'.

Vegetarianism went hand in hand with other reforming campaigns of the era – teetotalism, women's suffrage, 'back to the land' movements, rambling and cycling, experiments in communal living and campaigns to make clothing less ornate and restrictive. It also attracted members of the Aesthetic Movement, the Romantic poets and the Pre-Raphaelites, along with religious campaigners who argued for animal-friendly interpretations of the Bible, pseudo-scientific food 'hygienists' who advocated fasting and enemas, pacifists who claimed that eating meat was liable to 'inflame the passions' (not considered a good thing), and all kinds of radical thinkers. No wonder vegetarians were called 'cranks' – to this day, the word 'vegetarian' is used in a slightly derogatory way by some less enlightened types.

Active, committed vegetarians were in a tiny minority in the country, but they were vigorous and enthusiastic. Vegetarian cafés and health spas sprang up, and the Society ran cookery classes and holiday camps, and published pamphlets of advice and recipes, as well as a journal which has been in print continuously from the 1840s until the present.

Wartime dealt a double blow to vegetarianism. First, it was considered to be linked to pacifism and, by extension, to cowardice and unpatriotic behavior. Second, the fact that meat was rationed meant that it became a very desirable commodity, and meat-free meals signified poverty and desperation. After World War Two, meat rationing remained in place until 1954.

MENU

Curried parsnip soup

•

Crispy beer-
battered tofu

•

Crushed minted peas

•

Trifle

But by the late 1960s, vegetarianism was popular again. British pop music took over the world, and American-style hippie 'flower power' flooded across England. The Beatles were at the epicenter of this movement, setting the agenda for others to follow, and when they returned from a sojourn in an Indian ashram to announce that they had decided to go vegetarian, the impact on the popularity of the movement was huge. Health food shops found a new lease of life as young people came in search of alternatives to the standard British 'meat and two veg', and began demanding brown rice and yoghurt.

Vegetarianism's radical roots reappeared when it became associated with the modern 'animal rights' movement and campaigns against cruel industrial farming methods, hunting and vivisection. Today, veganism is gaining popularity, and interest in vegetarianism increases with every food-related 'scare' – 'Mad Cow Disease' made many people rethink their diets. Sir Paul McCartney continues to spearhead the movement with his Meat Free Mondays initiative. While some people still regard vegetarians as legitimate figures of fun, many others are eating less meat, or cutting out red meat. Vegetarianism is both an expression of individuality and a conscious acceptance of responsibility for one's own health, the health of the planet and global food sustainability. Being a vegetarian in England today is easy, with its multicultural society bringing a wealth of veggie-friendly culinary delights from every corner of the world, strict food labeling laws and a widely used Vegetarian Society 'Approved' logo.

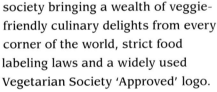

ENGLAND

Curried parsnip soup

Parsnips are venerable old English vegetables. Only the arrival of potatoes from America in the late 16th century dented their popularity. This recipe brings the humble parsnip up to date by adding some Indian flavors. Indian food is extremely popular in England, with many nominating curry as the national dish.

Ingredients

4 parsnips

1 carrot

1 onion

¼ cup / 50 g butter

½ tsp turmeric

½ tsp ground cumin

½ tsp curry powder

½ tsp chili powder

4 cups / 1 litre vegetable stock

Salt and pepper, to taste

Single cream, to garnish (optional)

Method

Peel the parsnips, carrot and onion, and chop them all into small pieces. Melt the butter in a large saucepan. Stir in the spices and cook for a minute before adding the chopped vegetables. Cook over a medium heat for 10 minutes, stirring frequently. Add the vegetable stock, bring to the boil and then simmer, covered, for 10-15 minutes, until all the vegetables are meltingly soft. Allow the soup to cool a little before transferring it to a blender and liquidizing until perfectly smooth. Reheat to serve, seasoning with salt and pepper to suit your preference. Swirl a little cream into each bowlful for an elegant presentation.

ENGLAND

Crispy beer-battered tofu

The English have been eating battered, fried fish for a very long time but, in the 1860s – when trawler fishing and railways brought abundant, cheap, fresh fish to the cities – stalls and restaurants selling fish and chips really took off. These days, overfishing of the seas around Britain has put many species of fish at risk, so even non-vegetarians may soon find themselves looking for a tasty, crispy alternative. I think this vegan version, using firm tofu marinated in a seaweed-flavored stock, fills the bill.

Ingredients

2 packs (approx 24 oz / 700 g) firm tofu

3 cups / 750 ml warm vegetable stock

3 tbsp soy sauce

Juice and zest of 1 lemon

6 tbsp dulse flakes

For the batter:

1 cup / 250 ml light vegan beer

1 cup / 110 g plain white flour, plus extra for dredging

Salt and pepper to taste

Method

Drain the tofu and press it with kitchen paper to remove excess moisture. Be as firm as you dare, without breaking it. Tofu is like a sponge, but will not suck up any flavors if it is waterlogged. Slice it into strips about ⅜ inch / 1 cm thick and pat it dry again.

Arrange the tofu strips in a large flat dish and pour over the warm stock, soy sauce, lemon juice and zest, and dulse flakes. Leave to marinate for several hours, or overnight. Turn the tofu pieces over once or twice if you get the chance.

Preheat the oven to 375°F/190°C and line a baking tray with parchment. Lift the marinated tofu slices out of the marinade and lay them onto the parchment – don't pat them dry or shake off any excess moisture. Bake them for 15 minutes, then turn them over and bake for a further 15 minutes.

Make the batter by whisking the beer into the flour, and season the mixture generously with salt and pepper.

Now set up your assembly line: first, the tofu pieces, then a plate covered with plain flour, then the bowl of batter and finally a large frying pan filled with vegetable oil to a depth of approximately ⅜ inch / 1 cm. Heat the pan until a drop of batter sizzles as soon as it hits the oil. Take a piece of tofu, dredge both sides in the flour, then dunk it into the batter and immediately place it in the frying pan. Be generous with the batter – the idea is to get a lot of crispy bits! Repeat the process until the pan is full, and fry the tofu, turning once or twice, until it is crisp and golden. Serve it as soon as you can, or keep it on a baking tray in a warm oven to stop the batter from going soggy.

Crushed minted peas

Mushy peas are traditionally served with fish and chips. They're something of an acquired taste – not everybody enjoys the watery consistency or the bland flavor. The dish was traditionally made with dried marrowfat peas and is a relative of the pease pudding in a traditional English nursery rhyme: 'Pease pudding hot, pease pudding cold, pease pudding in the pot, nine days old.' Not very appealing. This is a much fresher, tastier dish!

Ingredients

1 lb / 450 g fresh or thawed frozen peas

3 tbsp good-quality olive oil

3 tbsp chopped fresh mint

Juice and zest of half a lemon

Salt and pepper to taste

Method

Put the peas onto a flat worksurface and bash them with a rolling pin. Take care, they will try to escape. You should aim to crush them all, but not to reduce them to a pulp. Scoop them into a saucepan and add the olive oil, mint and salt and pepper. Cook them gently for 5 minutes, then stir in the lemon juice and zest, taste the mixture, and add more salt and pepper according to your taste. Serve warm, as a side dish.

ENGLAND

Trifle

Trifle has always been a problem for vegetarians, because of the jelly, which is traditionally made with gelatine. It's even more of a problem for vegans, because of the layers of custard and cream! I've devised a vegan version which could take pride of place on any tea table.

Ingredients

For the jelly:

1 pack strawberry-flavored vegetarian jelly crystals

4 oz / 110 g fresh strawberries

For the custard:

3 cups / 750 ml soy milk

Custard powder (see method)

Sugar (see method)

For the cream:

²/₃ cup / 160 ml soy milk

1¹/₃ cups / 320 ml rapeseed oil

2 tbsp agave nectar

1 tsp vanilla extract

Toasted flaked almonds, to decorate

Method

For the jelly: I'd strongly recommend buying a pack of strawberry- or raspberry-flavored vegetarian jelly crystals, even if you have to get them via the internet. It's possible to make vegetarian jelly using gelling agents like agar agar and carrageen, but it can be tricky to work out how to flavor it with fruit juice without its becoming too diluted to set. Citrus juices and high-fat recipes can also cause setting problems, and agar agar tends to become opaque and rather unpleasantly firm when it sets. Make the jelly by adding boiling water according to the directions on the packet. Rinse the strawberries, pat them dry and slice them in half if they are big ones. Arrange them in the base of a heat-proof glass dish. Pour the liquid jelly on top and let it cool a little, then pop it into the fridge to firm up.

For the custard: Ready-made vegan custard is not ideal for a trifle, as it tends to stay runny. Custard powder was invented in 1837 by Alfred Bird, whose wife was allergic to eggs, and it's perfect for vegans (as long as you don't add dairy milk!). Use 3 cups / 750 ml of non-dairy milk and check the packet to find out how much custard powder and sugar you should add. Let it cool, but not so much as to become really firm or get a skin, then pour or spoon it carefully over the jelly, smooth the top and return the bowl to the fridge.

For the cream: For a really good trifle, you need thick, spoonable cream, not the runny kind. Having done a few experiments, I think the following technique, which is a bit like making mayonnaise, works best. You'll need a goblet-style liquidizer and may have to divide your ingredients to make two or three batches of the cream, depending on the capacity of your equipment.

Put the soy milk, vanilla and agave nectar into the liquidizer, put the lid on and set the motor running. Very slowly, drizzle the oil into the mix – there should be a hole in the lid to let you do this. Be patient – when the mixture emulsifies you'll hear the tone of the motor change as the cream suddenly starts to thicken. When it is thick, spoon it over the set custard layer of the trifle and decorate it with a handful of toasted almond flakes. Chill the whole thing again before serving.

Ethiopia

Ethiopian food reflects centuries of tradition, and authentic Ethiopian dining requires not only some complex spice blends but also awareness of the intricate social rituals associated with a meal. Paying attention to the detail is extremely rewarding – not only will you experience the full flavors of traditional Ethiopian food, you will also have fun sharing the communal meal with family and friends.

The Christian Coptic Church was declared a state religion in Ethiopia in 330CE, and it remains very strong today. Most people eat according to the dictates of the religion. There are many 'fast days', including every Wednesday, every Friday and the 55 days of Lent (Tsom), during which consumption of meat and dairy are prohibited. This means that it is relatively straightforward to find vegan food in the country.

Ethiopian wats or stews are generally flavored with *berberé*, a complex blend of up to 15 spices with hot chili, and a spiced clarified butter called *niter kibbeh*. Ethiopian cuisine is the hottest and most highly spiced in Africa – this may be one reason why Ethiopian restaurants are becoming popular in the West. Less spicy stews made without berberé are called *alecha*.

A traditional meal consists of a selection of *wats*, served on *injera*, a very large and spongy pancake. Take note, if you are planning to make these in the authentic way, you'll need to start several days before your guests are expected, as the method involves a natural fermentation process. Injera is made with teff, a tiny ancient grain which is

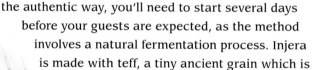

now attracting interest in the West because it is gluten free. It's not uncommon to create a base for a meal by overlapping a number of these pancakes. The meal is enjoyed communally – after washing their hands (another religious ritual which can involve the server splashing water onto the guests' hands from a decorative jug, but might be done with wet wipes!), guests use their right hands to tear off small pieces of injera and use them to scoop up the wat. It is considered a sign of friendship to feed others by hand in this way – say 'Goorsha' as you pop the food in. The larger the piece of food involved, the stronger the friendship!

Meals might be served with *tej*, a honey wine, or *tella*, a home-made beer, but there is no tradition of dessert. However, the Ethiopian coffee ceremony is well worth including in your plans if you are treating guests to an Ethiopian-style dining experience. Ethiopians drink home-roasted coffee after every meal, several times a day, and each time it is served according to this complicated but delightful ritual. Coffee is often said to have been discovered in Ethiopia when a goat-herd noticed his goats looking surprisingly lively. He took the berries they had eaten to the local monks, who viewed them with suspicion and threw them onto the fire. The aroma that resulted was irresistible, and the rest is history.

MENU

Berberé paste

•

Niter kibbeh (Ethiopian spiced butter)

•

Injera (savory pancakes)

•

Atakilt wat (vegetable stew)

•

Ye'abesha gomen (Ethiopian spicy greens)

•

Misr wat (lentil stew)

•

Coffee ceremony

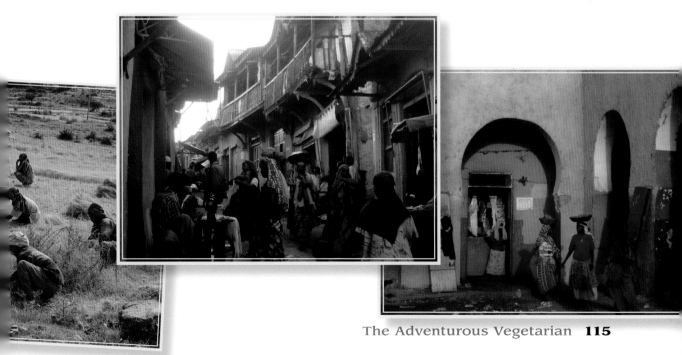

Berberé paste

It's well worth making a batch of this aromatic spice paste – you do need a lot of ingredients (and possibly a dedicated coffee grinder!) but it's not a lengthy or unpleasant job. The paste will last for a week in the fridge – you can also freeze small portions of the paste, or just grind the spices and chili to a powder and use that instead – it will keep for a long time in a spice jar.

Ingredients

The 'whole' spices:

3-4 whole dried chilis

1-2 tsp dried red pepper flakes

2 tsp cumin seeds

1 tsp cardamom seeds

1 tsp fenugreek seeds

8-10 black peppercorns

6 allspice berries

4 cloves

The ground spices:

1 tbsp paprika

1 tbsp salt

1 tsp ground ginger

1 tsp turmeric

1 tsp cayenne

½ tsp nutmeg

The 'wet' ingredients:

1 onion, chopped

3 cloves garlic, crushed

½ cup / 125 ml vegetable oil

4 tbsp water or red wine

Method

Put the whole spices into a heavy-bottomed frying pan and warm them gently. Stir them to stop them burning. When they begin to offer up their aromatic oils, take the pan off the heat and transfer the spices onto a cool plate to stop them from cooking any further.

If you are cooking on gas, use tongs to hold the whole dried chilis over the flame and toast them lightly. Don't scorch them, as you might do if you were going to peel a bell pepper – the idea is just to warm them up so that they become soft and flexible. Then chop them roughly and discard the stems and seeds.

Put the toasted whole spices and chopped chilis into a coffee grinder and grind to a powder. (After this, you might decide to keep a coffee grinder specifically for grinding freshly toasted spices!)

At this point the powder can be stored or you can put it into a food processor with all the remaining ingredients and process to a smooth paste.

Niter kibbeh
(Ethiopian spiced butter)

This spiced, clarified butter is used a great deal in Ethiopian cooking, and adds a wonderful depth of flavor. To make a version that can be used in vegan dishes, use vegetable oil instead of butter. Warm the oil very gently and follow the recipe as if you are using melted butter – there will not be any solids to scoop away.

Ingredients

1 lb / 450 g unsalted butter

½ onion, chopped

2-3 cloves garlic, crushed

A hand of ginger root, sliced ¼ inch / ½ cm thick

4 cardamom pods

1 cinnamon stick

4 cloves

1 tsp fenugreek seeds

½ tsp turmeric

Method

Melt the butter in a small pan, over a gentle heat. Stir in all the rest of the ingredients and heat on the lowest possible setting for approximately an hour. Resist the temptation to stir, so that the butter milk solids settle into the bottom of the pan. Carefully pour the clear golden liquid through a sieve lined with muslin, into a bowl or jug, leaving the solids in the bottom of the pan – discard these and the ingredients that have been strained out. Allow the butter to cool and store in the refrigerator until needed.

Clarified butter has a longer 'shelf-life' than fresh butter – the process was developed in India to stop fresh butter from spoiling in the heat, and technically Indian ghee can be kept for several months without refrigeration – it behaves like an oil. Any trace of milk solids or water will affect this, however, so for this home-made version, I'd recommend keeping it chilled and using it within a month, just in case.

ETHIOPIA

Injera (savory pancakes)

The ancient and authentic method of making injera requires only ground teff (teff flour), water and a little salt. The magic ingredient is time. Leaving the teff batter to sit, at room temperature, for up to 3 days means it is exposed to natural airborne wild yeasts. Once these have colonized the batter, fermentation begins and this produces the bubbles that give the pancakes their spongy consistency.

Ingredients

350 g ground teff (teff flour)

1 litre water

Salt, to taste

Vegetable oil, for frying

Method

Mix the teff and water to make a batter, and leave it in a bowl, loosely covered with kitchen paper, at room temperature, for up to 3 days until it starts to bubble and smells sour. When you are ready to cook the pancakes, season the mixture with a little salt. Heat a little oil in the largest frying pan you own (non-stick is best here), and pour in sufficient batter to make a thick pancake. Cook gently and watch carefully as bubbles appear on the surface of the pancake and the batter quickly dries out and firms up. The cooking time is very short – the pancakes should not be browned at all, and they are only cooked on one side. Allow them to cool before serving, but don't stack them as they can stick together and the trapped steam will make them gummy.

To serve, either give each guest an individual plate lined with injera and topped with wats, or use several injeras, overlapping, to form a large communal 'plate'. Blob a selection of wats in front of each guest, and serve any left-over injera on the side, folded. Guests should wash their hands, then use pieces of the injera served on the side to begin scooping up the wat. When the injera served on the side are gone, it's time to make a start on the injera underneath the wat, which will have absorbed lots of spicy juices from the food. Be sure to make your injeras quite thick so that the topping doesn't leak through!

Atakilt wat (vegetable stew)

Doro wat, made with chicken, is probably the most popular dish in the country. This version uses all the same spices with some chunky zucchinis/courgettes. You'll need your home-made berberé and niter kibbeh – for a vegan version, be sure to use vegetable oil instead, and leave out the hard-boiled eggs, of course.

Ingredients

6 zucchinis/courgettes, trimmed and cut into bite-sized chunks

Juice of 1 lemon

2 tsp salt

2 onions, chopped

3 cloves garlic, crushed

1 tbsp grated fresh ginger

4 tbsp oil, butter or niter kibbeh

2 tbsp paprika

4-8 tbsp berberé paste (depending on how spicy you want it to be)

¾ cup / 175 ml stock

4 tbsp red wine

1 tsp cayenne (more if you dare)

Salt and pepper to taste

4 hard-boiled eggs, shelled (optional)

Method

Put the zucchini/courgette chunks into a large bowl and toss with the lemon juice and salt.

Put the onions, garlic and ginger into a food processsor and blend to a paste, adding a splash of water if necessary.

In a large saucepan, warm the oil, butter or niter kibbeh, stir in the paprika and cook for 1 minute. Stir in the berberé paste and cook for 2 more minutes. Stir in the onion-garlic-ginger paste. Fry gently until most of the moisture has evaporated away.

Add the zucchinis/courgettes, stock or water, wine, cayenne and salt and pepper. Stir everything together thoroughly, bring the mixture to a boil and then reduce the heat, cover the pot and simmer for 25 minutes. Check the mixture occasionally – you may need to add a splash more water to prevent it from sticking. The consistency should be like a thick sauce. If you are using the hard-boiled eggs, mix them into the dish just before serving. Take off the shells, but leave the eggs whole – you'll be expected to break them up when you eat the dish by pinching them in a folded piece of injera.

ETHIOPIA

Ye'abesha gomen (Ethiopian spicy greens)

Here's the perfect use for your home-made niter kibbeh!

Ingredients

4 tbsp niter kibbeh

4 tbsp olive oil

1 large onion, finely chopped

3 cloves garlic, crushed

2 chilis, deseeded and finely chopped

A 'thumb' of fresh ginger root, grated

7 cups / 700 g shredded greens (cabbage, kale, chard etc)

Salt and pepper, to taste

White wine vinegar, to taste

Method

Melt the niter kibbeh gently in a large pan, then add the oil and the onions. Turn up the heat and fry the onions until they are browned. Stir in the garlic, chilis and ginger and cook for a further 3 minutes. Add the shredded greens to the pan, toss well with the oil and add $1\frac{1}{3}$ cups/325 ml of boiling water, and salt and pepper. Bring back to the boil, then cover and cook on a very low heat until the greens are tender. Serve hot, on injera, with the wats.

Misr wat (lentil stew)

Using your home-made niter kibbeh and your berberé paste can turn a humble lentil stew into something very special indeed.

Ingredients

4 tbsp niter kibbeh

1 small onion, finely chopped

4 cloves garlic, crushed

2 tbsp berberé

1⅓ cup / 200 g red lentils

1 small tomato, cored and chopped

Salt, to taste

Method

Melt the niter kibbeh gently in a medium-sized saucepan, and fry the onions until they are golden. Add the garlic and fry for a few seconds before adding the lentils, half of the berberé, the chopped tomato and 4 cups / 1 litre of water. Reduce the heat and simmer for about 40 minutes, until the lentils have disintegrated. Stir the mixture occasionally to make sure it doesn't stick to the bottom of the pan and burn – add a splash more water if necessary. Just before serving, stir in the rest of the berberé and season with salt.

ETHIOPIA

The Ethiopian coffee ceremony

No Ethiopian meal is complete without coffee, and it is prepared and served in a very specific way. Without some traditional equipment, you may only be able to achieve an approximation of the effect, but it is still fun to try!

In many households, the coffee-making apparatus is kept in a special position, surrounded by aromatic grass. The ceremony is, where possible, carried out by a young woman dressed in a traditional white dress with a colorful woven trim. She begins by burning some frankincense, making the room slightly smoky and wonderfully aromatic. She will then take a handful of green coffee beans (it's possible to buy these via the internet!) and put them into a small, flat pan. She begins to heat the pan over a small charcoal stove and adds a little water, gently agitating the beans to remove any husks when the water is poured away. She continues to roast the beans until they are black and beautifully fragrant. At this point she will carry the hot pan around the room, wafting the aroma towards guests who in turn murmur their appreciation. But the coffee is still a long way off, and guests are often served dry snacks such as plain fresh popcorn or peanuts, while they wait.

The woman carrying out the coffee ceremony now pounds the beans using a pestle and a long-handled mortar. Next they are put into a distinctively shaped black clay coffee pot called a *jebena*, and covered with boiling water. More time passes as the hostess repeatedly pours and strains the coffee, and then allows the remaining sediment to settle at the bottom of the pot.

At last, the coffee is poured, in a steady stream and from some height, into tiny china cups without handles. (Vegans beware, sometimes the spout of the coffee pot is stuffed with horsehair to strain the coffee as it is poured!)

It is traditional to make one more cup than there are people waiting to drink. Each cup will be prepared beforehand with plenty of sugar (or, in some rural districts, salt). The coffee is served black. As the guests enjoy this first round of coffee (*abol*) the hostess tops up the coffee pot with more hot water, and soon a second round is poured (*tona*). Finally, a third round is poured (*baraka*) – it is considered most impolite not to stay for a third cup, at least. The ceremony is carried out three times a day, after every meal, and is a social event when people gather to chat about the events of the day, local goings-on, politics and scandals.

France

France is synonymous with fine dining – in fact, it's difficult to talk about top-quality food at all without resorting to French words like gourmet, chef, restaurant, menu and cuisine! At the height of their power, the French aristocracy demanded extremely high standards from their household chefs and the endless round of house parties became a showcase for each chef's work, with some serious competition going on, and money no object. The French Revolution of 1789 changed everything. There were no longer any great houses that required great chefs, and those talented individuals found themselves not only out of work, but in many cases, on the run, as they were closely identified with the despised aristocracy. As a result, many fled the country. Arriving in neighboring countries, including England, they naturally sought the employment that they were used to, but few households were large or lavish enough to make use of them. The skill of creating gourmet meals for large amounts of people, night after night, seemed to be redundant. It was at this moment in history that the French restaurant was born. The French as a nation remain extremely proud of their cuisine, which tends to be based around meat, rich sauces and extravagant desserts.

Unfortunately, the strong traditions of French cuisine tend to make life very difficult for vegetarians. France today is one of very few Western countries where a request for food without meat can be met with outright derision – going without meat is widely considered to be absurd. *The Vegetarian* magazine in the UK regularly receives reports from travelers who have struggled to obtain vegetarian food in France, faced with restaurateurs who thought a little meat wouldn't matter, or that by using their home-made rich beef stock they would be giving the vegetarian diner a treat. One recent report described a French waiter's response to '*Je suis végétarienne*' as one of immense sorrow and sympathy, as if the diner had confided information about a life-threatening illness.

The Association Végétarienne de France, launched in 1994, has an uphill task but is working hard to promote vegetarianism in France. Françoise Degenne is a member of its Board who looks after the recipe pages in its magazine as well as organizing cookery classes in her home town, Tours. She writes:

Although their number is steadily increasing, vegetarians are still a very small minority of the French population. Being vegetarian is not always easy, but nowadays health-food shops and some online stores offer a very good range of products for both ovo-lacto vegetarians and vegans.

Restaurants are a different matter, but things are gradually improving there too. Even restaurants that carry no vegetarian dishes on their menu will often gladly prepare one to oblige a customer, especially if contacted in advance. The tourist industry has helped in this regard, with visitors spontaneously requesting vegetarian options.

Catering in school canteens and the like is more complicated, and this is a problem that the Vegetarian Association of France is tackling, in partnership with other associations. It is difficult to change mentalities, particularly in a country as proud of its gastronomic tradition and reputation as France is. The majority of the population remains convinced that a meal without meat is not a meal and that vegetarians are malnourished and complicated individuals. Dieticians are backward in presenting the scientific facts about the advantages of a vegetarian diet.

The reality on the ground is quite different, however. Awareness of the ecological, health and humane reasons for reducing one's meat consumption is definitely growing. The French Vegetarian Association is increasingly sought out for information and advice for new vegetarians.

Association Végétarienne de France
vegetarisme.fr

These French vegetarian dishes were contributed by Laura Bourichon (**http://vivalim.free.fr/**) and Ôna Maiocco, whose blog includes lots more French recipes that are suitable for vegans (**foodwaytogreenheaven.com/wordpress**).

MENU

Chicory in walnut cream sauce

•

Mushrooms and béchamel in puff pastry

•

Tofu with mustard sauce

•

Tarte aux pommes (apple tart)

FRANCE

Chicory in walnut cream sauce

A raw food dish that remains loyal to French culinary tradition.

Ingredients

$^2/_3$ cup/ 50g walnuts

1 tbsp rapeseed oil

1 tbsp cider vinegar

2 small heads of white chicory

1 apple

Salt and pepper

Method

Soak the walnuts in water overnight. The next day, drain them and put half of them into a food processor with the rapeseed oil, cider vinegar and 2 tablespoons of water. Process until smooth and creamy.

Wash the chicory and cut it horizontally into ½-inch / 1-cm wide strips. Put it into a serving dish. Chop the remaining walnuts roughly, and add to the dish. Wash, core and slice the apples and add these. When you are ready to serve, pour the creamy sauce over the top and mix through gently.

FRANCE

Mushrooms and béchamel in puff pastry

Ingredients

1 packet of ready-rolled puff pastry
 (check the label to see if it is vegetarian or vegan)

2 tbsp olive oil

1 cup / 240 ml soya milk, plus extra for brushing

¼ cup / 25 g plain flour

2 oz / 50 g mushrooms, finely chopped

Salt, pepper and nutmeg

Method

Warm the olive oil in a frying pan. Sprinkle in the flour, salt, pepper and nutmeg. Gradually add the soya milk, stirring constantly and vigorously, to avoid lumps. Bring the mixture to the boil – this will thicken your sauce. You may need to stir constantly over a medium high heat for several minutes. Set aside and allow to cool.

Preheat the oven to 355°F/180°C.

Cut the puff pastry into circles around 4 inches / 10 cm in diameter – you will need two for each person. Place 1 teaspoon of cooled béchamel sauce and 1 teaspoon of mushrooms on half of the circles. Cover with the remaining pastry circles, and press around the edges with the tines of a fork to seal. If this creates a ragged-looking edge, carefully trim to a neat circle with a sharp knife. Brush the tops with a little soya milk and transfer to a baking sheet lined with baking parchment. Bake for 20-25 minutes or until golden.

Serve with green salad or with a handful of cherry tomatoes roasted on the vine.

FRANCE

Tofu with mustard sauce

Ingredients

1 lb / 450 g French beans

7 oz / 200 g extra firm smoked tofu, sliced

1 tbsp olive oil

1 shallot, finely chopped

1 vegetable bouillon cube diluted in 3 tbsp boiling water

¾ cup / 200 ml soya cream

1 tsp Dijon mustard

2 tbsp finely chopped chives

Salt and pepper

Method

Steam the French beans for 20 minutes.

In a dry frying pan, cook the tofu for a few minutes on each side. Set the cooked tofu aside, wipe the pan and then heat the olive oil and fry the chopped shallots until they are golden. Add the vegetable bouillon and continue to cook until all the water is evaporated. Add the soya cream and mustard and cook gently for 5 minutes. Remove from the heat and stir in the chives, salt and pepper.

Poor the mustard sauce over the tofu and French beans to serve.

FRANCE

Tarte aux pommes (apple tart)

There are some French classics that are suitable for vegetarians! This version of the classic apple tart is suitable for vegans too. The sweet pastry is kneaded to make it firm and crisp.

Ingredients

For the pastry:

2 cups / 200 g wholemeal flour

⅔ cup / 100 g vegan margarine

1 tbsp / 20 g sugar

3 tbsp /40 ml water

For the filling:

⅓ cup / 30 g cornflour

2½ cups / 600 ml soya milk

¼ cup / 30 g vegan margarine

⅓ cup / 80 g sugar

1 tbsp vanilla essence

For the top:

3 or 4 sweet apples

1 tbsp sugar

Method

Preheat the oven to 390°F/200°C.

To make the pastry, sift the flour into a bowl. Add the margarine and sugar and rub with the tips of your fingers until the mixture resembles fine breadcrumbs. Gradually add the water to make a soft dough. Knead the dough on a lightly floured surface until smooth and elastic, then form into a ball. Roll out the pastry into a circle that is about ⅛ inch / 3 mm thick. Use the dough to line a 10-inch / 27-cm loose-bottomed fluted tart tin, prick the base all over with a fork and bake blind for 5 minutes. Take the tart out of the oven and turn the temperature down to 355°F/180°C.

To make the filling, put the cornflour into a small bowl and whisk in 4 tbsp of the soya milk. Set aside. Put the rest of the soya milk and the margarine into a small saucepan and bring to the boil. Sprinkle the flour and sugar onto the mixture and whisk it in. Cook the mixture over a medium heat, whisking constantly, for 5-6 minutes or until thickened. Remove the saucepan from the heat, add the cornflour mixture and vanilla essence and whisk well to combine. Pour the filling into the cooked pastry case.

Peel, core, and cut the apples into very thin slices. Arrange the apple slices in concentric circles over the tart. Overlap them well as they will shrink a little during baking. Sprinkle the sugar over the apples. Bake for 30 minutes.

Ghana

Ghanaian food tends to be arranged around a starchy staple, which makes it problematic to transfer to a Western kitchen. Millet, maize and beans are easy enough to obtain, but cassava, sorghum and taro are not, and even if you are lucky enough to find a supply, the traditional preparation method is very daunting. It involves pounding the vegetables in a very large bowl or bucket with a very heavy stick until they are worked into a sticky dough. *Fufu* is pounded cassava and plantain, or pounded taro. *Banku* (or *akple*) is a cooked fermented maize dough. *Kenkey* (or *dokonu*) is a fermented maize dough, wrapped in corn husks or plantain leaves and cooked into firm balls.

By all accounts, these are not particularly palatable to the Western traveler, and as you are not 'allowed' to chew fufu, getting it down can be more of an ordeal than a pleasure. For that reason, I've chosen something more familiar for this chapter – sticky rice balls (*omo tuo*). Rice is not grown in Ghana but has become very widely used and popular.

The starchy part of the meal is typically accompanied by fried or smoked fish and often a hot sauce made from red and green chilis. Milk and dairy products were not widely consumed until relatively recently, because tsetse flies and the diseases that they spread made it very difficult to keep cattle. To thicken soups

MENU

Avocado with
peanut dressing

•

Nkate nkwan
(peanut soup)

•

Omo tuo (rice balls)

•

Muhallabia
(ground rice pudding)

and stews, the cuisine relied upon ground pulses, seeds and peanuts. In theory this makes Ghanaian cuisine quite vegan-friendly – in practice, meat of all kinds is added to soups and stews as available, and bushmeat, snails, offal, trotters and cow skin all go into the pot.

Originally brought to the country from South America by Portuguese traders, peanuts are now a local crop and widely used – the peanut soup or stew (*nkate nkwan*) suggested here is enjoyed in many variants across West Africa. Rural communities keep hens for eggs and meat, but the term 'garden egg' means a vegetable similar to an aubergine or eggplant. Palm oil is a key ingredient in many stews including Red Red, a popular bean stew that takes its name from the rich color of the oil.

Fresh fruits, especially oranges and mangoes, are plentiful in season and sweet dishes are made with peanuts, ripe plantain, condensed milk – and with kube toffee, made from coconuts.

GHANA

Avocado with peanut dressing

Ingredients

3 tbsp shelled peanuts

½ tsp paprika

½ tsp cinnamon

Cayenne, to taste

Salt, to taste

2 avocados

1 tbsp lemon juice

Fresh chives

Method

Wrap the peanuts in a clean dish towel and crush them with a rolling pin. Transfer to a small bowl and mix with the paprika, cinnamon, cayenne and salt. Peel and stone the avocados, chop them into bite-sized pieces and sprinkle with the lemon juice. Sprinkle the peanuts over the avocados and chill. Top with fresh chopped chives just before serving.

Nkate nkwan (peanut soup)

Widely enjoyed across West Africa, this soup may contain fish or meat and can take the form of a thick stew or a thinner soup. In Ghana is it often served with rice balls. This recipe makes a hearty and nutritious vegan soup (check the ingredients of the peanut butter as some brands contain dairy products).

Ingredients

1 onion

1 red bell pepper

3 cloves garlic

1 tbsp olive oil

14 oz / 400 g canned chopped tomatoes

2 pints / 1 litre vegetable stock

¼ cup / 50 g uncooked white long-grain rice

6 tbsp peanut butter

Pepper and dried red pepper flakes, to taste

Method

Peel and chop the onion. Peel, deseed and chop the pepper. Peel and crush the garlic. Fry them gently in the olive oil until slightly browned, about 5 minutes. Add the tomatoes, stock and seasoning, and simmer for 10 minutes. Stir in the rice, cover the pan and simmer for 20-25 minutes, until the rice is soft. Add the peanut butter and stir well, over a low heat, until it has melted into the mixture. Serve hot – add a couple of rice balls to each bowl to make this into a substantial meal.

GHANA

Omo tuo (rice balls)

Ingredients

¾ cup / 150 g long-grain white rice

2 pints / 1 litre water

Salt, to taste

Method

Put the rice, water and salt into a heavy-bottomed pan, bring to the boil, reduce the heat to a bare simmer. Cover and simmer for 20-25 minutes until the rice is cooked and most of the liquid has been absorbed. Remove the pan lid and continue to cook gently until there is no free moisture in the pan (stir frequently to make sure it doesn't burn). Remove from the heat and allow to cool.

When the rice is cool enough to handle, use a potato masher to mash it into a smooth paste. Shape the mixture into 8 balls. It's very sticky and it helps to have wet hands when you're doing this, so keep a bowl of water close by. Take care – the mashed rice holds its heat for a long time and it may be hotter under the surface than you think! Pop the rice balls on top of bowls of steaming soup to serve.

GHANA

Muhallabia (ground rice pudding)

A deceptively simple dish, made sublime with fragrant rosewater.

Ingredients

2 tbsp ground rice

1 tbsp cornflour

2 pints / 1 litre milk

5 tbsp sugar

2 tbsp rosewater

1 cup / 70 g ground almonds

Chopped pistachios, to garnish

Grated nutmeg, to garnish

Method

Mix the ground rice and cornflour with a little of the milk to form a paste. Gently heat the rest of the milk in a large pan. Add the sugar and mix well to combine. Add the rice paste to the warm milk, stirring continuously, and bring the mixture to just below boiling point. Maintaining this temperature, keep stirring until the mixture thickens (about 10 minutes). Reduce the heat to a bare simmer and stir in the rosewater and ground almonds. Cook gently for a further 5 minutes, then remove from the heat and allow to cool a little before transferring to small serving bowls. Chill and garnish with the chopped pistachios and nutmeg before serving.

Grenada

Known as the Spice Isle, Grenada produces a third of the world's nutmeg as well as other spices including cinnamon and vanilla, cocoa and exotic fruits. Modern Grenadian cuisine is carefully spiced and prepared with great attention to detail and presentation. There is also a thriving tradition of street food, although this is mostly barbecued meat and fish.

Mark Hardy runs The Lodge in Grenada, a vegan guest-house which is often described as an 'oasis' for vegetarians visiting the Caribbean. Mark writes:

Generally speaking, vegetarianism is not widely practiced in the Caribbean. The 'protein myth' abounds – it's hard to persuade people that it's possible to live without eating meat. Having said that, not many Caribbeans eat red meat – chicken is by far the most popular meat, and in Grenada people do use soya and TVP (textured vegetable protein) products extensively. The notable exception, of course, are the Rastas who (assuming they are following the Rastafarian faith, and not what we call here 'rent-a-dreads') are mostly vegan. Amongst the majority of the population of these islands, however, vegetarianism is considered somewhat unusual and veganism is most certainly anathema.

MENU

Coo Coo with spicy
tomato relish and
plantain

•

Oildown

•

Coconut ice

Oildown, the main dish in this menu, is the Grenadian national dish. It usually contains meat but I have veganized it. The Jamaican national dish is Salt Fish and Akee – it's not so easy to veganize this! Akee is a tree fruit with a bright red bell-shaped shell/skin that opens when ripe to reveal (usually) three creamy yellowish-white brain-shaped soft fruit. There is a red string or vein in each fruit that must be removed as it is poisonous. It's not popular in Grenada because of this potential hazard (although there is no real danger provided one is diligent!). Akee has a wonderfully original soft texture and a refined nutty taste – it can be eaten raw with salads or thrown in at the last minute to any cooked dish. It also makes the best vegan scrambled eggs imaginable. Unfortunately I imagine that it would be almost impossible to purchase fresh outside the Caribbean, and the canned version is ghastly!

Mark Hardy
The Lodge – Grenada
thelodgegrenada.com

GRENADA

Coo Coo with spicy tomato relish and plantain

Ingredients

Coo Coo:

1 cup / 150 g cornmeal (polenta)

13½ fl oz / 400 g can coconut milk

½ green bell pepper, finely diced

½ red bell pepper, finely diced

Salt and freshly ground
  black pepper

Nutmeg

Tomato relish:

2 tbsp tomato paste/purée

2 onions, chopped

2 cloves garlic, crushed

11 oz / 300 g fresh tomatoes, chopped

A handful of Shadow Benny (fresh basil)

Salt and black pepper

2-3 tbsp coconut oil

Plantain:

1 plantain

Coconut oil

Salt

Method

Preheat the oven to 350°F/180°C.

For the Coo Coo:
Pour the coconut milk into a medium-sized pan and bring it to the boil. Reduce the heat to a simmer and season to taste with salt, pepper and nutmeg. Gradually pour in the cornmeal and stir or whisk continually until the mixture thickens. Take the pan off the heat and add the finely diced bell peppers.

For the tomato relish:
Sauté the onion and garlic gently in the coconut oil for 2-3 minutes, then stir in the chopped tomatoes and cook on a gentle heat until the tomatoes begin to break down, about 5 minutes depending how ripe they are. Stir in the tomato paste/purée and basil, and season to taste with salt and pepper.

For the plantain:
Peel the plantain and slice it into ⅛-inch / 1-cm thick pieces. Fry it gently in the coconut oil until crisp and golden on both sides. Serve warm with the Coo Coo stacks.

To assemble the dish:
Grease four 2½-inch / 6-cm baking rings thoroughly and place them on an oiled baking tray. Put a medium-sized spoonful of the coo coo polenta mixture into each ring. Spread the mixture out using the back of a spoon to make a smooth base for each stack. Top the polenta with a spoonful of tomato relish and spread to the edges of the ring so that the tomato relish will show up nicely when the stacks are removed from the rings. Continue to alternate polenta and relish layers, ending with a polenta layer. Brush the tops with a little oil and bake for 20 minutes. Loosen the stacks with a knife before gently easing the stacks out of the rings and onto serving plates. Serve with a few freshly cooked plantain slices and more tomato relish.

GRENADA

Oildown

Mark writes: 'Oildown is the national dish of Grenada. It is a one-pot meal of what are locally called "provisions", normally cooked over an open fire. It usually contains meat or fish, but my version is vegan.' Any combination of root vegetables can be used but this simple recipe is an ideal excuse to visit a shop or market stall that stocks West Indian vegetables and experiment with some new flavors. The quantities are variable, depending on what you find and how many people you want to feed! The coconut milk separates during cooking, with the watery part sinking to the bottom of the dish and simmering to make steam that cooks the vegetables, and the oily part moving to the top of the dish, helping to stop it from drying out as it cooks. As a result, the finished dish can look rather oily – look for a low-fat variety of coconut milk if you would prefer to cut down the oiliness... but the dish isn't called Oildown for nothing!

Ingredients

Breadfruit	Breadnut (or cooked chestnuts)
Dasheen	Coconut milk
Yam	Onion
Sweet potato	Salt
Calaloo (or spinach)	Black pepper
Bluggoe (a starchy cooking banana)	Turmeric
Plantain	Thyme

Method

Wash, peel and slice all the vegetables. The calaloo (or spinach) can be washed and left whole. Layer all the ingredients in a large heavy-bottomed casserole dish with seasoning, turmeric and thyme between each layer. Cover the vegetables with coconut milk, bring to the boil and gently simmer until all the liquid is absorbed – if it starts to get dry before the vegetables at the top are cooked, you may need to add more coconut milk. You should be able to slice the finished result. Mark says: 'This is not easy to present elegantly, but tastes fabulous!'

Coconut ice

You'll need a food processor that can crush ice cubes to make this refreshing dessert.

Ingredients

2 x 13½ fl oz / 400 g cans of coconut milk

4 tbsp caster sugar

4 tbsp desiccated coconut

15 cardamom pods

Method

Set aside 2 tbsp of coconut milk and leave in the fridge to chill. Pour the remaining coconut milk into ice cube trays and freeze until solid.

Crush the cardamom pods, save the seeds and discard the pods. Grind the seeds to a rough powder using a pestle and mortar. (It's possible to buy cardamom powder, but the coarsely crushed seeds add texture and color to this dish.)

Put the frozen cubes of coconut milk into the bowl of a food processor with the sugar, desiccated coconut and ground cardamom seeds. Process to a grainy powder (something like snow!), then add the chilled coconut milk and blend to a soft sorbet. Serve immediately, with some chopped banana or mango for a truly Caribbean dessert.

India

India is home to more vegetarians than any other country in the world, and the wide variety of dishes available to vegetarians and vegans there has already filled many books. Nitin Mehta, founder of the Young Indian Vegetarians (youngindianvegetarians.co.uk), writes:

'India is a haven for vegetarians! Every eatery will have a big choice of vegetarian food. If you arrive in a place like New Delhi you might find it difficult to find many exclusively vegetarian restaurants in the city center but there will be plenty of them in the suburbs. Almost all the mouth-wateringly good street food is vegetarian.

'As you travel by road in India you will come across roadside food outlets called *dhabas* which serve amazing, piping hot vegetarian food. It is safe to eat this food as it is prepared fresh. Most Hindu, Sikh and Jain places of pilgrimage serve strictly vegetarian food, in many cases free of charge. Most Hare Krishna temples have a restaurant called Govinda's and the food is great.

'Western vegetarian food is widely available, as is the Indian vegetarian version of Chinese food. For a few dollars you can eat like a Maharaja and if you are having a Thali you will have to beg them to stop serving any more food! In India, eggs are not considered vegetarian but Indians are big on dairy products so vegans have to be more careful, particularly of *ghee* (clarified butter) and *paneer* (a kind of cheese often used in vegetarian curries). Vegetarian, eggless food is labeled on packaging with a green circle in a green square. The word for vegetarian is *shakahari* – just mention that word and they will understand! Most cities have animal welfare groups so, if you have a look on the internet before you go, you might be able to make contact with like-minded people.'

Nitin kindly put me in touch with Jigyasa Giri and Pratibha Jain, Indian cookery writers who have published award-winning books on their vegetarian

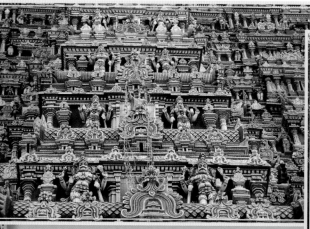

culinary inheritance and on the principles of ayurvedic cookery. Jigyasa and Pratibha faced an enormous challenge in trying to devise a menu that encompassed tastes and styles from all over India! Their careful choices draw on culinary traditions from the north, south and east of the country and together make up a meal rich in colors, flavors and textures. You can find out more about these generous women and their books at pritya.com.

Diana Ratnagar of Beauty Without Cruelty (India) also made contact, and kindly drew my attention to the free vegan recipe database at bwcindia.org. Bhuvaneshwari Gupta, a vegan who works for PETA in India (**petaindia.com**), wrote: 'India is considered the birthplace of vegetarianism and about 31% of the people in India are vegetarian. Vegetarian food is available at just about every restaurant and can easily be made vegan. Tofu and soy milk are widely available. Recent studies suggest that 20-25% of North Indians and approximately 70% of South Indians may be lactose intolerant, so it's easy to see why the demand for dairy-free options is growing rapidly.'

Indian vegetarian food could be the subject of a lifetime's study! If you've never applied yourself to making authentic Indian vegetarian food from scratch at home, this menu is the perfect place to start.

MENU

Fruit sandesh

•

Ajwain roti

•

Pea and potato koftas

•

Paneer capsicum subzi

•

Kosumbari
(cucumber) salad

•

Perugu pachchadi
(spiced yoghurt with
vegetables)

•

Dal with palak

•

Pistachio and
almond kulfi

INDIA

Fruit sandesh

A sweet dish from Bengal, made with *chenna* (curdled milk) and fresh fruit. Serve chilled at the beginning of your meal. If you don't have citric acid crystals, use a tablespoon or two of fresh lemon juice to curdle the milk. The choice of fresh fruit is yours – I have made this dish successfully with kiwi fruit, plums and strawberries.

Ingredients

4 cups / 1 litre milk

¼ to ½ tsp citric acid crystals

¼ cup / 50 g caster sugar

½ tsp rosewater

A few strands of saffron

A pinch of cardamom powder

1 cup / 150 g of finely chopped mixed fruit

Rose petals (if available), to decorate

Method

To make the chenna, dissolve the citric acid in 1 tbsp water and set aside. Bring the milk to a boil and then switch off the heat. After 5-10 minutes, add half of the citric acid solution, stir gently and cover with a lid. Within a couple of minutes, the milk will curdle, separating quite cleanly into the milk solids and the whey, which should be quite clear. If the mixture is still cloudy, add the rest of the citric acid solution. Strain the curdled milk through a fine muslin cloth and press it down gently so that the whey is completely removed from the chenna. (The whey can be discarded or used in roti dough – if you are making the rotis in this menu too, keep the whey.)

Put the chenna onto a clean worksurface, add the sugar, rosewater and saffron, and knead gently. The sugar crystals will dissolve and the mixture will become soft. Add the finely chopped fresh fruit and continue to knead until everything is well mixed. Roll the mixture into lemon-sized balls and flatten gently. Make a depression in the center to place a rose petal, if you can get any – otherwise, decorate with some larger fruit pieces. Arrange the sandesh balls on a tray and sprinkle the cardamom powder on top. Chill before serving.

Photo top right, page 157.

Ajwain roti

You'll probably need to visit an Indian food store to find carom seeds (ajwain), but they add a delicious authentic flavor to these dainty breads – it would be a shame to miss it.

Ingredients

2 cups / 250 g plain wholewheat flour

¼ tsp carom seeds (ajwain)

¼ cup finely chopped fresh mint leaves

½ cup / 125 ml milk or home-made whey (see fruit sandesh recipe opposite)

A pinch of salt

Ghee (clarified butter) – for frying

Method

Make a soft dough with 1½ cups / 190 g of the wholewheat flour, along with the carom seeds, mint leaves, salt and milk or whey. Add a little water if you need it, and work in a teaspoon of ghee towards the end of the kneading process to smoothen the dough. Cover and set aside for 10-15 minutes.

Divide the dough into 10-12 equal portions and roll into balls. Use the remaining flour to sprinkle over a board, then flatten one ball and, with a rolling pin, roll it into a circle around 6 inches / 15 cm in diameter. Dust off any excess flour and transfer the roti onto a hot skillet over a medium heat. Within seconds, small bubbles will appear on the surface. Flip the roti using a pair of tongs, and increase the heat to high. Brush the roti with a little ghee on both sides and continue to cook until the surface is browned and crisp. Repeat with the remaining dough, and serve hot.

Photo bottom right, page 157.

INDIA

Pea and potato koftas

A perennially popular dish from Punjab; a spicy potato-pea mixture coated with batter and deep fried. Gram flour is made from garbanzos/chickpeas and may also be called *besan*.

Ingredients

Vegetable oil – for deep frying

For the batter:

1½ cups / 150 g gram flour

1 tbsp rice flour

½ tsp red chili powder

¼ carom seeds (ajwain)

A pinch of turmeric powder

A pinch of bicarbonate of soda

Salt, to taste

For the stuffing:

4 medium-sized potatoes

1 cup / 110 g peas

1 large onion, finely chopped

1 tsp chili powder

1-2 green chilis, finely chopped

½-inch / 1-cm piece of ginger, finely chopped

½ tsp dried mango powder (*amchur*)

¼ tsp garam masala

2 tbsp pomegranate kernels (optional)

Salt, to taste

Method

Peel the potatoes, boil them, mash them and allow to cool. Boil the peas, crush them coarsely and mix into the mashed potato. Add the remaining stuffing ingredients (except the pomegranate) and mix thoroughly.

Heat 1 tbsp oil in a wok, add the potato mixture and fry for 7-8 minutes. Allow the mixture to cool and stir in the pomegranate, if you want to use it. Divide the mixture into ten equal portions and roll into balls.

Make the batter by beating all the ingredients together thoroughly with 2 cups / 500 ml of water.

Fill a wok or deep saucepan to a depth of around 4½ inches / 12 cm. Heat it until a drop of batter sizzles as soon as it comes into contact with the oil. Dip the potato balls in the batter to cover them completely, then carefully drop into the hot oil. Lower the heat and cook the koftas, turning them occasionally, until they are evenly cooked and golden. Serve hot as a snack or an accompaniment to a meal.

Photo also top left, page 156.

Paneer capsicum subzi

You can buy ready-made paneer, or make your own. Use the method in the fruit sandesh recipe on page 154 to curdle some milk, then after you have strained it, wrap it tightly in a muslin cloth and let it sit under a weighted plate for 30 minutes to firm up. 4 cups / 1 litre of milk typically yields 4½ oz / 130 g of paneer so you'll need 8 cups / 2 litres for this recipe. You could also use firm tofu.

Ingredients

9 oz / 260 g paneer

2 large red bell peppers

2 onions

2 large carrots

2-3 tbsp vegetable oil

½ tsp cumin seeds

2 green chilis, finely chopped

1 inch / 2.5 cm root ginger, finely chopped

1 tsp chili powder

1 tbsp ground coriander

A pinch of turmeric powder

1 tsp ground cumin

4 tbsp tomato paste/purée

Salt, to taste

Method

Chop the paneer, peppers, onions and carrots into bite-sized pieces. Warm the oil in a large pan and add the cumin seeds. Cook for a moment before adding the chopped onions, green chilis and ginger. Sauté gently for 2-3 minutes. Add the chopped carrot and pepper, and cook for a further 2-3 minutes. Now stir in all the remaining spices, the salt and the tomato paste/purée. Cook for 2 more minutes. Finally, stir in the paneer and cook for one more minute. Serve right away with rotis.

Photo bottom right, opposite,
and top middle, page 156-7.

INDIA

Kosumbari (cucumber) salad

This cooling salad is known as *kosumbari* in Tamil Nadu. The split black gram used for the tempering is also called *urid dal*.

Ingredients

½ cup / 3 oz split mung beans

1 large cucumber, peeled and finely chopped

1 green chili, finely chopped

1 tsp lemon juice

½ tsp sugar (optional)

Salt, to taste

1 tbsp desiccated coconut

Fresh cilantro/coriander leaves, to garnish

For the tempering:

¾ tsp split black gram (husked)

¾ tsp mustard seeds

1 tbsp vegetable oil

Method

Soak the split mung beans in lukewarm water for 1 hour. Strain and set aside. (Discard the water or use it to make the dal from this menu.)

Mix the soaked beans with the chopped cucumber, green chili, lemon juice, sugar and salt.

In a wok, heat the oil for tempering. Add the split black gram and as it turns golden, stir in the black mustard seeds and let them pop. Pour the tempering over the cucumber and garnish with the coconut and chopped coriander leaves. Serve chilled, as an accompaniment to the meal.

Photo top, page 161,
and left middle, page 156.

Perugu pachcadi (spiced yogurt with vegetables)

This dish is known as *perugu pachchadi* in Andhra Pradesh. Asafetida is a pungent white powder – it smells of sulfur or rotten eggs but don't worry, it tastes all right! It's often used to season food where religious laws forbid the use of onions and garlic. Make sure you store it in a tightly sealed jar as it can taint other foods stored nearby. Use desiccated coconut if you can't get fresh coconut meat for the paste. Grinding the ingredients is best done with a pestle and mortar or an electric spice grinder – the quantities are too small to work in a food processor.

Ingredients

2 cups / 500 ml thick plain yogurt

1 carrot

1 onion

1 large tomato

Salt, to taste

For the paste:

½ tsp black mustard seeds

1-2 tbsp fresh grated coconut

1 green chili – whole, with stalk removed

1-inch / 2.5-cm piece of ginger

2 tbsp chopped fresh cilantro/coriander leaves

½ tsp asafetida powder

For the tempering:

3 tsp vegetable oil

1 heaped tsp split black gram, husked (see note on cucumber salad opposite)

1 heaped tsp black mustard seeds

2 red chilis, nicked at the tail, with stalks retained

2 green chilis, slit, with stalks removed

5-7 fresh curry leaves, with stem

¼ tsp asafetida powder

Method

Chop the carrot, onion and tomato into thin, 1-inch / 2.5-cm long pieces or ½-inch / 1-cm cubes. For the paste, chop the chili and the ginger, and soak the mustard seeds in a little water for half an hour. Strain and grind, along with the other ingredients of the paste, to a fine consistency.

Put the yoghurt into a large bowl and mix in the paste, vegetables and salt.

Heat the oil in a wok for tempering. Add the black gram; as it turns golden, add the black mustard seeds and cook until they pop. Reduce the heat and stir in the chilis, curry leaves and asafetida. Cook for 1 more minute, then garnish the yoghurt mixture with this crunchy tempering. Serve as a side dish.

Photo left, page 165, and right middle, page 157.

Dal with palak

A simple dal with lentils, tomatoes and spinach, from Rajasthan. If you can't get ghee, it's easy to make your own: melt 1 lb / 450 g of butter in a pan, bring it to the boil, then scoop off any bubbly bits on the surface and let it cool. The milk solids should collect in the bottom of the pan, and the oil should be clear and golden. Carefully pour off the oil and discard the milk solids. Let the oil sit in a cool place until it solidifies, then store it like butter.

Ingredients

1 cup / 200 g split red lentils

3 large tomatoes, quartered

½ tsp fenugreek seeds

¼ tsp turmeric powder

A generous handful of fresh spinach leaves, washed and finely chopped

½ tsp sugar

Salt, to taste

Fresh cilantro/coriander leaves – for garnishing

For the tempering:

2 tsp ghee

½ tsp black mustard seeds

¼ tsp asafetida powder

½ tsp cumin seeds

10-12 curry leaves (fresh leaves, complete with the stem, if you can get them)

1 heaped tsp chili powder

Method

Put the lentils into a large saucepan with the tomatoes, fenugreek seeds and turmeric powder. Cover with water and simmer for 30 minutes, mashing the tomatoes occasionally, until the lentils are soft and disintegrating. Beat the mixture with a wooden spoon to break the lentils down further and make a smooth paste.

In a deep pan, melt the ghee and then cook the mustard seeds gently until they pop. Stir in the asafetida powder, cumin seeds, curry leaves and chili powder and cook for a minute, then add the spinach leaves and sauté for 2 minutes. Add the sugar, salt and cooked lentils. Stir in enough water to give the mixture a soupy texture, switch the heat to high and allow the dal to boil for 5-6 minutes. Serve hot, garnished with cilantro/coriander leaves, with steamed rice or rotis.

Photo bottom right, opposite,
and bottom left, page 156.

Pistachio and almond kulfi

Kulfi is like Indian ice cream, but because it is generally made as a custard and then frozen solid, rather than being churned like Italian ice cream, it is relatively dense. The ground almonds in this recipe also contribute to the slightly firmer texture. Kulfi is often frozen in small conical molds – if you can't get these, serve it in scoops or use small robust glasses, ramekins or coffee cups as molds. The hardest part about this recipe is cooking the milk – make sure you keep stirring it, as it will stick to the bottom of the pan, and if you turn your back for a moment, it's certain to boil over, so choose a time when you are going to stay in the kitchen for a while. This recipe was kindly contributed by Mohana Gill, who also wrote the recipes for the Malaysia chapter.

Ingredients

4 cups / 1 litre milk

8 tsp sugar, or to taste

½ tsp ground cardamom seeds

1 tbsp shelled pistachios, thinly sliced

1 tbsp ground almonds

Method

Put the milk into a wide, heavy pan and bring to the boil over a high heat, stirring constantly. Now lower the heat and cook the milk, stirring constantly, until it has thickened and reduced to about 1¾ cups – this will take about 40-45 minutes. Use a rubber spatula to scrape the milk off the sides of the pan and stop the dried milk from burning. When the milk is sufficiently reduced, stir in the sugar, pistachios, almonds and ground cardamom seeds, stir well, and allow to cool.

Pour the mixture into kulfi molds or small ramekins, wrap in plastic wrap or foil and freeze until set, about 6 hours. To serve, remove the ice cream from the molds by running a sharp knife around the edges of the kulfi – you might also find it useful to run them briefly under a hot tap. Slip each kulfi on to a dessert plate, cut into pieces if you like, and serve at the end of your Indian meal.

Ireland

Ask anybody which food they associate most closely with Ireland and they will say 'potatoes'. There is a widespread belief that the Irish, in years gone by, subsisted on very little except potatoes. In a famously green and fertile land, that seems strange until you learn two things.

First, in the mid-19th century, a great deal of the farmland was owned by British aristocrats, absentee landlords who used the land to grow grain for export. And second, under British Protestant rule, Irish Catholics were not allowed to purchase land, being limited instead to renting small plots on which to grow food.

An acre of land could produce enough potatoes to feed a family for a year – growing sufficient grain for the purpose would have required much more space. By 1845, about 50% of Ireland's population was reliant on potatoes for food – and in that year, the harvest was devastated by blight. Starvation and disease quickly took hold. By 1850 the population of Ireland had been reduced by a quarter due to death and mass emigration.

Today, Ireland remains a relatively agricultural country. Only 9% of its agricultural land is used to grow crops – 91% is grassland or rough pasture, used for beef and dairy farming. Irish cheesemaking has enjoyed a resurgence in recent years, with new and traditional varieties made by small independent producers attracting praise from lovers of fine food, whether vegetarian or not. For vegetarians, the jewel in Ireland's crown is probably Café Paradiso, chef Denis Cotter's vegetarian restaurant in Cork, which produces world-class innovative vegetarian cuisine with its roots firmly connected to the local smallholders and cheese-makers who supply the essential fresh ingredients.

Maureen O'Sullivan is the Secretary of the Vegetarian Society of Ireland (vegetarian. ie), and kindly supplied the recipes for this chapter. She writes:

When you ask people whether it's easy to be a vegetarian in Ireland, I think there's likely to be a huge generational difference in the responses. These days, younger people are spoiled for choice! I gave up meat and fish definitively between 1979 and 1982, and things were quite difficult back then, but the food scene here has improved dramatically. Estimates suggest that about 1% of the population is vegetarian, we have a Vegetarian Society of Ireland, and most towns have meet-up groups that eat out together regularly. Most large cities cater quite well, with several all-vegetarian and even vegan restaurants, and there is a growing trend for non-veggie restaurants to produce special vegetarian or vegan menus.

Generally speaking, restaurants are quite helpful. This may be partly due to the need to accommodate allergy sufferers, but also, culturally, in this country it is acceptable to be a fussy eater. Vegans will find it more difficult than vegetarians in traditional restaurants due to the widespread use of dairy both in soda bread, as a dressing for vegetables and in desserts. However, we have a wide variety of ethnic restaurants whose cuisine is often vegetarian or vegan and vegetarian convenience foods are widely available.

There is, of course, a tendency for people to classify fish as a vegetarian food, and Parmesan often also gets included in the vegetarian options, in spite of the fact that it is never suitable for vegetarians because of the requirement that it is made using animal rennet. We are working to educate restaurants on such matters and most are very open to learning. More and more people are starting to understand the links between diet and health. There can be a bit of teasing about dietary preferences but, if we see this from Gandhi's perspective, at least we are no longer being ignored or laughed at – we are being fought a little and in the next stage, we will win!

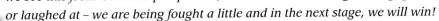

IRELAND

Spinach and potato bake

Ingredients

4 medium potatoes, peeled

½ pound / 250 g fresh spinach, washed, dried and chopped

1 clove garlic, crushed

½ cup / 125 ml vegan milk, plus extra for brushing

3 tbsp chopped fresh mixed herbs

Sea salt and white pepper to taste

Pinch nutmeg

1 tbsp nutritional yeast flakes (optional)

2 tbsp sunflower oil, for greasing

Method

Cut the potatoes in half and boil them in salted water for 10-15 minutes, until they are softened but not fully cooked. Drain and slice thinly.

Preheat the oven to 355°F/180°C.

Mix the spinach, garlic, milk and herbs. Season with salt, pepper and nutmeg. Lightly grease a baking dish with sunflower oil. Layer the potatoes and spinach mixture, starting and ending with a layer of potatoes. Brush the top with some vegan milk and put in the oven to bake for 30 minutes.

Allow to cool in the dish for a few minutes before serving.

IRELAND

Irish stew

Ingredients

2 tbsp sunflower oil

2 leeks, cleaned and sliced

2 onions, diced

1 parsnip, sliced

2 carrots, sliced

1 large potato, cut into chunks

2 turnips, peeled and sliced into chunks

2 celery sticks, diced

2 pints / 1 litre vegan or vegetarian vegetable stock

$^2/_3$ cup / 150 g pearl barley

2-3 tbsp fresh parsley, chopped

A few sprigs each fresh rosemary, fresh thyme and fresh marjoram

Salt and pepper to taste

Method

Sauté the leeks and onions in the oil in a large soup pot until translucent. Add the remaining vegetables and stir to coat the vegetables with oil for a few minutes.

Add the stock, barley and parsley to the pot. Tie the sprigs of fresh herbs together with a piece of cooking string and add to the pot. Bring to the boil, then reduce heat and simmer for an hour, or until the vegetables are tender and the stew has thickened, adding more water if necessary. Remove the herb bundle.

Season with salt and pepper and serve with soda bread.

IRELAND

Soda bread

This quick and easy rustic bread is traditionally made with buttermilk – this version with vegan yoghurt works just as well.

Ingredients

½ lb / 225 g plain wholemeal flour

½ lb / 225 g plain white flour

1 tsp baking powder

½ tsp bicarbonate of soda

9 oz / 250 g unsweetened vegan soy yogurt

2 tsp dried mixed herbs

1 tbsp olive oil

Soy milk

Method

Preheat the oven to 390°C/200F. Grease a baking sheet and dust with a little flour.

In a large mixing bowl, mix all the dry ingredients together and then stir in the yogurt and oil, along with sufficient soy milk to give the mixture a slightly wet consistency. Do not knead, but transfer to the baking sheet straight away. Shape into an oval, flattish shape and use a sharp knife to cut a cross in the center – this helps the bread to expand in the oven. Bake for 45-50 minutes and allow to cool before slicing.

IRELAND

Blueberry pancakes

Ingredients

3 heaped tbsp buckwheat flour

½ tsp baking powder

4½ oz / 125 g soya yogurt, fruits of the forest flavor

Soy milk, to adjust consistency

A generous 1 cup / 125 g blueberries

Oil, for frying

Method

Mix the flour and baking powder together in a bowl. Mix in the yogurt and add sufficient soy milk to give a slightly runny consistency. Gently stir in the blueberries.

Heat a large non-stick frying pan on a medium to low heat and either add some sunflower oil or spray with low-calorie oil spray. Fry small amounts of the batter to make pancakes around 3 inches / 8 cm in diameter. Keep the heat low so that the blueberries don't burst straight away – the pancakes are pretty with purple juice if the berries burst, but the taste is nicer if they burst in your mouth! Maureen recommends serving these with maple syrup and vegan vanilla ice cream.

Israel

Suzanne Barnard, *Director of the Jewish Vegetarian Society (jvs.org.uk), writes about her experience of vegetarianism in Israel.*

Israel is one of the easiest places in the world to be vegetarian. The country's Mediterranean climate allows for the production of a great variety of cheap fresh fruit and vegetables. Across Israel there are kibbutzim, collective communities traditionally based on agriculture, and if you visit one of these you might easily end up picking avocados, dates, grapefruit, olives, oranges and more.

According to a 2001 survey conducted by the Ministry of Health, Israel has the world's second largest percentage of vegetarians after India, with 8.5% of adults following a meat-free diet. While there are no more recent formal statistics, my impression is that these numbers are growing and that veganism is also becoming more and more popular. Being vegetarian is certainly not an unusual choice nor frowned upon in Israel.

Israel's cuisine is unique due to the country's diverse population. People from many different countries, with many different foods and customs, live there. A great number of Eastern European Jews arrived in 1948, bringing with them traditional Jewish dishes that they had cooked in countries such as Hungary, Poland and Russia. The Palestinians, the majority of whom were of Arab descent, enjoyed a cuisine fused from the Middle East and North Africa.

Most typical Israeli dishes are derived from Arab cuisine. These include numerous varieties of *hummus* (mashed garbanzo/chickpea dip) – Israelis love to debate which hummus restaurant is the best (currently, Abu Hassan in Jaffa and Lina in East Jerusalem claim the crown). *Falafel* (deep-fried garbanzo/chickpea balls) is the ultimate vegetarian fast food, and is very popular with all Israelis – vegetarians and non-vegetarians. *Ful* (broad beans) is a typical Egyptian food,

MENU

Carrot and
cabbage salad

•

Sabich
(pita, egg and salad)

•

Rugelach (cream
cheese pastries)

often eaten along with hummus or as a separate dish. *Tahini* (a savory spread made from ground sesame seeds) – also from Arab cuisine – is very popular. It can be added to any dish, or enjoyed as a sauce with pita or other bread, in one of its many varieties, including 'green tahini' (with lots of parsley). Local Arab cuisine also offers dishes such as *tabuli* (bulgur wheat salad), *mejadarah* (rice with lentils), stuffed vine leaves and eggplant/aubergine dishes. Many Arab sweets are vegan.

Immigrants have also introduced vegan dishes into Israeli cuisine. From Yemen came *jachnun* and *melawach*; from North Africa, *couscous*; from Kurdistan, *kubeh*. There are also many Ethiopian vegan dishes. Besides all these, many vegetarians eat Western-style meat-equivalents, which are available in many supermarkets and in a growing number of specialized restaurants in the bigger cities.

The Jewish dietary laws (*kashrut*) inadvertently aid vegetarians. The Torah tells us not to 'boil a kid in its mother's milk'. Keeping kosher therefore means that dairy and meat products cannot be stored in the same place, prepared using the same dishes, or eaten at the same time. All dishes at 'kosher dairy' restaurants are strictly meat-free (though fish is not considered to be meat), all wine is vegetarian and cheese does not contain animal rennet. By the same token, in 'kosher meat' restaurants, or whenever meat is served at communal meals, all other food must be strictly dairy-free. As a consequence, non-dairy margarine and non-dairy milk are widely served and sold across Israel, which is really useful for vegans.

ISRAEL

Carrot and cabbage salad

Ingredients

9 oz / 250 g green or red cabbage, shredded finely

6 oz / 180 g carrots, grated

1 scallion/spring onion, finely chopped

A few lettuce leaves, shredded

2 tbsp raisins

2 tbsp flaked almonds

2½ tbsp sunflower oil

Juice of ½ lemon

1 tsp celery salt

Salt and freshly ground black pepper, to taste

Slices of orange, to garnish

Method

Combine the grated carrots, cabbage, spring onion, lettuce leaves, nuts and raisins and mix well.

Mix together the oil, lemon juice, celery salt, pepper and a little water, and pour the dressing over the salad.

Garnish with slices of orange.

Serve cold.

Sabich (pita, egg and salad)

This is street food that attracts a cult following, along with lots of arguments about the perfect toppings. Some people add hummus, some add tahini, some add both. Some feel a smear of spicy harissa paste is essential, others advocate different hot sauces. Some add pickles or chopped avocado. But the ingredients that never change are the chopped tomato and cucumber salad, the fried eggplant/aubergine and the boiled egg slices. My version includes a bright yellow salsa of finely chopped mango and mouth-puckering preserved lemon, and I wouldn't eat Sabich without it!

Ingredients

4 large pita breads

For the mango and lemon salsa

1 just-ripe mango

1 small preserved lemon

2 tsp harissa paste

For the chopped salad:

3 fresh tomatoes

½ cucumber

3 scallions/spring onions

3 tbsp chopped fresh flat-leaf parsley

Juice of half a lemon

4 hard-boiled eggs, peeled and sliced

2 large eggplants/aubergines

Vegetable oil, for frying

4 tsp harissa paste

Hummus and/or tahini, to taste

Method

Make the mango and lemon salsa first. It's best with a mango that isn't too ripe, so that it's sweet but tangy, and holds its shape. Peel and stone the mango and chop it finely. Chop the lemon very finely and mix them together with the harissa paste.

Make the chopped salad: trim and chop the scallions/spring onions, chop the tomato and cucumber finely and stir them up together with the lemon juice and chopped parsley.

Slice the eggplant/aubergine around ¼ inch / ¾ cm thick and shallow-fry it in the oil. Don't rush it; you're aiming for soft, oily and well browned rather than crisp.

Warm or toast the breads and place each onto a serving plate. Smear casually with harissa, then pile on the chopped salad, eggplant/aubergine, egg slices, hummus, tahini and mango salsa at random! Tuck in while the bread and eggplant/aubergine are still warm.

ISRAEL

Rugelach (cream cheese pastries)

These popular pastries are made with a soft dough enriched with cream cheese. The filling given here is a traditional favorite but there's really no end to the possibilities – try filling them with chocolate spread or chopped chocolate and nuts.

Ingredients

½ cup / 100 g cream cheese

⅔ cup / 100 g unsalted butter (at room temperature)

6 tbsp granulated sugar

½ tsp vanilla extract

A pinch of salt

1 cup / 100 g plain white flour

1 tbsp light brown sugar

1 tsp ground cinnamon

½ cup / 50 g raisins

⅔ cup / 50 g finely chopped walnuts

4 tbsp apricot jam (sieved or pureed if it is very lumpy!)

1 egg, beaten with 1 tbsp milk

Method

Cream the cheese and butter together, then stir in 1 tablespoon granulated sugar, the vanilla and the salt. Gradually add the flour and mix until just combined. Gather the dough into a soft ball and cut in half. Wrap each piece in cling film and chill for an hour.

Make the filling: stir together 3 tablespoons of granulated sugar, the brown sugar, half the cinnamon, the raisins and the walnuts.

Unwrap one of the dough balls and place it on a floured board. Roll it into a circle around 10 inches / 25 cm in diameter. Spread two tablespoons of apricot jam over the surface and scatter half of the filling mixture on top. Cut the circle into 12 wedges – first cut it into quarters and then carefully cut each quarter into three equal wedges. Roll up each wedge, as tightly as you can, starting with the wide edge. It doesn't matter if some of the filling spills out – part of the appeal of these pastries is that they show off their sticky filling!

Repeat the process with the second piece of dough to create 24 rolled-up pastries. Arrange them on a parchment-lined baking tray. Chill for 30 minutes and preheat the oven to 355°F/180°C.

Mix the remaining 2 tablespoons of granulated sugar with the remaining cinnamon. Brush the pastries with the egg and milk, and sprinkle with the cinnamon sugar. Bake for 15-20 minutes until golden and oozing. Allow to cool (at least a bit!) before tucking in.

Lebanon

Lebanese cuisine is an eclectic combination of typical Mediterranean fare with Middle Eastern influences. It does not rely heavily on meat – the most common non-vegetarian ingredients are fish, poultry and lamb. Bread is consumed at virtually every meal, and used to scoop up food instead of a spoon or fork. Bread has a special place in the hearts of the Lebanese and in some Arabic dialects it is called *esh* – literally meaning 'life'. Yoghurt and *labneh* (strained yoghurt) are popular, but butter and cream are rarely used, and most dishes are cooked in large amounts of olive oil, with plenty of garlic and fresh seasonal herbs.

Lebanese food is influenced by the terrain – there are snow-capped mountains, fertile valleys where grape vines, wheat and olives flourish, and sun-drenched beaches – but it's also influenced by the geographical position of the country. A natural meeting point for traders and travelers between Europe and the Middle East, it's a cultural crossroads and the popular style of eating, sharing many different small dishes, reflects the welcoming and hospitable attitude of the people. The Lebanese are natural travelers, and have tended to bring back the dishes they found on their travels, so today you can expect to find burgers and sushi alongside more traditional food in the main towns and cities. The influence of the Ottoman Turks is behind the enduring popularity of lamb, baklava and yoghurt.

MENU

Fattoush salad

•

Fasolia bi zait
(pinto bean and
potato stew)

•

Potato kibbeh

•

Sfouf (semolina cake)

There's also a noticeable French culinary influence which dates back to a period of French control under a United Nations Mandate which was in place between the end of the First World War and 1943 – hence the Lebanese penchant for pastries, sauces and Arak, a potent anise-flavored spirit originally devised to replace the French Absinthe after it was withdrawn from public sale. Thick, Arabic-style coffee is also very popular, often spiced with ground cardamom and served with sweet desserts.

The national dish of Lebanon is *kibbeh*, traditionally made by pounding fresh raw lamb to a paste with a pestle (*modaqqa*) and mortar (*jorn*) and then kneading it with spices and bulgur wheat. George Lassalle, an English food writer, observed this unpleasant sight and reported that it was 'frightening'! Although lamb is the traditional main ingredient, these days there are hundreds of variations, including plenty of vegetarian and vegan-friendly versions such as the potato-based baked kibbeh included in this chapter.

LEBANON

Fattoush salad

There are many, many versions of this dish – all of them include bread, but opinions vary on whether it is best fresh and soaked in olive oil, brushed with oil and baked, or fried. Although bread is an essential ingredient, the other constituents of the salad vary: typically it contains tomatoes, cucumber, radishes, scallions/spring onions and fresh parsley and mint, but red and green bell peppers and sundry other salad ingredients may also make an appearance. By tradition, the greens in the dish are purslane leaves, but these might not be easy to find – Little Gem or Romaine lettuce will do the job. Apart from the bread, the other essential in the dish is sumac, a lemony spice that adds a tart kick to this substantial salad. Strong lemon flavor features in many Lebanese dishes and it can be quite a shock to Western palates. This salad dressing also contains pomegranate molasses, a sweet-sour tangy syrup that has become a store-cupboard staple in my kitchen.

Ingredients

8 cherry tomatoes

½ cucumber

4 radishes

8 scallions/spring onions

2 tbsp fresh chopped mint

2 tbsp fresh chopped flat-leaf parsley

1 Romaine lettuce or 2 Little Gem lettuces

For the bread:

3 wholemeal pita breads

4 tbsp olive oil

2 tsp sumac

For the dressing:

2 tsp sumac

2 tbsp lemon juice

1 tbsp pomegranate molasses

2 cloves garlic

3 tbsp olive oil

Method

Preheat the oven to 390°F/200°C. Prepare the bread: First, mix 4 tbsp olive oil with 2 tsp sumac in a large mixing bowl. Separate the pita breads into halves and cut or tear them into bite-sized pieces. Put them into the bowl and toss with the sumac and oil. Transfer to a baking tray and bake for approximately 5 minutes until beginning to color – they'll crisp up as they cool.

Make the dressing: peel and crush the garlic. Mix the sumac, garlic, lemon juice and pomegranate molasses together in a small bowl, then whisk in the olive oil.

Chop the tomatoes in half. Slice the cucumber and radishes, chop the scallions/spring onions and shred the lettuce. Chop the fresh herbs, but not too finely – they should still be recognizable in the dish. Toss all these fresh ingredients together in a large serving bowl. Immediately before serving, toss the dressing through the salad and stir in the bread.

LEBANON

Fasolia bi zait (pinto bean and potato stew)

This hearty stew has its origins in the mountainous regions of Lebanon. Be sure to use dried pinto beans as ready-cooked canned beans will not soak up the flavor of the dish, and will disintegrate before the cooking time is over. Cooking the dish for a long time over a low heat is important as it brings out the sweetness of the garlic and allows the potatoes to disintegrate and thicken the stew.

Ingredients

1 cup / 450 g dried pinto beans

1 onion

1 whole bulb of garlic

1 medium-sized potato

½ cup / 120 ml olive oil

2 tbsp tomato paste/purée

Salt, to taste

Method

Soak the dried beans overnight in cold water.

Peel and chop the onion and garlic. Peel the potato and cut it into very small dice. Put the oil into a large, deep pan, stir in the drained beans, onion, garlic and potato, and cook gently for 10 minutes, stirring frequently. Then pour 3 pints / 1½ litres of water into the pan and mix well. Bring to the boil and then reduce the heat to a bare simmer. Put a lid onto the pan and leave it to cook for an hour, stirring occasionally. Check that the beans are soft, then stir in the tomato paste/purée, increase the temperature and boil the stew for 10 minutes. Season with salt to suit your own taste. Serve hot with pita bread.

LEBANON

Potato kibbeh

A tasty vegan version of the Lebanese national dish. The cooking technique is somewhere between roasting and frying – the dish is drenched with oil and sizzles in the oven for an hour to become succulent and crisp. The character of this dish depends on the evocative scent and flavor of the Lebanese 7-spice – this is a mixture of equal quantities of ground nutmeg, ginger, allspice, cinnamon, cloves, fenugreek and black pepper.

Ingredients

1 cup / 150 g bulgur wheat

14 oz / 400 g canned garbanzos/chickpeas

3 medium-sized potatoes

1 cup / 100 g plain white flour

4 tbsp fresh chopped mint

4 tbsp fresh chopped parsley

6 scallions/spring onions

1 onion

1 tsp cayenne pepper

1 tsp Lebanese 7-spice

⅔ cup / 150 ml olive oil

Salt to taste

Method

Preheat the oven to 390°F/200°C.

Peel, boil and mash the potatoes. Rinse the bulgur wheat and leave it to sit in a sieve for 30 minutes. Drain and rinse the garbanzos/chickpeas, then wrap them in a clean dishcloth and bash them with a rolling pin. The idea is not to smash them to pieces but just to loosen the skins. Unwrap them and you should find that it is easy to slide off the skins by rubbing them between your fingers. Discard the skins and mix the crushed garbanzos/chickpeas with the mashed potato and bulgur wheat. Chop the herbs, scallions/spring onions and onion finely and add to the mixture. Stir in the cayenne pepper, Lebanese 7-spice and salt.

Put the flour onto a board, turn the mixture out and knead it, gradually incorporating the flour, until everything holds together as a firm dough. Press into a baking tin or dish, and smooth out – it should be about ½ inch / 1.5 cm thick. Using the tip of a sharp knife, cut the mixture into small squares. Pour the olive oil over the surface of the kibbeh, allowing it to seep into the dish. The oil should cover the surface of the kibbeh.

Bake the dish for 50-60 minutes, until the oil has been absorbed and the kibbeh is browned and beginning to crisp up. Serve hot or cold with pita bread.

LEBANON

Sfouf (semolina cake)

An easy, popular semolina cake that's perfect with coffee at the end of a Lebanese meal. Pine nuts are often used instead of almonds to decorate the top of the cake. A little turmeric adds distinctive color and flavor. It's useful to remember this recipe if you need to make a cake without eggs!

Ingredients

2 cups / 330 g fine semolina

1½ cups / 150 g plain white flour

½ tsp turmeric

1 tsp baking powder

1⅓ cups / 200 g butter

1¼ cups / 250 g sugar

1½ cups / 375 ml milk

½ cup / 50 g slivered almonds

Method

Preheat the oven to 355°F/180°C. Grease a shallow rectangular baking tin.

Mix the semolina, flour, turmeric and baking powder together in a large bowl. Melt the butter and, in a separate bowl, mix it with the sugar and milk, along with ½ cup / 120 ml of water. Pour the wet ingredients into the dry ingredients, mix well and spoon into the prepared tin. Smooth the top and sprinkle with the slivered almonds. Bake for 20 minutes until springy and golden. Allow to cool in the tin before turning out and cutting into small squares.

Malaysia

D r P Vythilingam, President of the Malaysian Vegetarian Society (which can be contacted at **vegetariansocietymalaysia.org**) kindly put me in touch with Mohana Gill, the author of two award-winning vegetarian cookbooks: *Fruitastic* (winner of the Gourmand Special Jury Award in 2007) and *Vegemania* (winner of the Gourmand 'Best Vegetarian Cookbook in the World' award in 2008). Both books stress the importance of fruit and vegetables as an essential foundation for health and longevity. Mohana generously shared many of her recipes, reflecting the Indian and Chinese influences on Malaysian cuisine as well as traditional Malay dishes.

Mohana writes: *'Eating is a national pastime in Malaysia and there is always delicious food to be found everywhere. There are three distinct ethnic groups in Malaysia – Malay, Chinese and Indian – and each has a characteristic style of food. Different Malay regions are all known for their unique or signature dishes. The main characteristic in traditional Malay cuisine is the generous use of spices. Coconut milk is also important in giving Malay dishes their rich, creamy character. Malay cooking also makes use of lemongrass and galangal. Nearly every Malay meal is served with rice. Food is eaten delicately with the fingers of the right hand.'*

I was initially surprised when Mohana offered me Indian and Chinese style recipes as well as Malay dishes, but visitors to Malaysia do have three distinct choices of cuisine.

Indian food in Malaysia generally has its roots in Kerala and Tamil Nadu, areas of south India which are quite veggie-friendly. Cheap south-Indian cafés offering 'banana leaf' or 'chettinad cuisine' offer good pickings. *Mamak* stalls and restaurants draw on Tamil Muslim culinary traditions, and although it is usually possible to find vegetarian and vegan options, their pre-prepared curry sauces often contain chicken or fish.

Chinese food is often prepared to order, which means that, in theory, diners can make any special requirements known. In practice, however, many of the stocks and sauces used in Malaysian Chinese restaurants contain non-vegetarian ingredients, and it can be hard to be sure what you are getting. High-end Chinese restaurants offer some fascinating fake meat products – there are even vegetarian frogs' legs, though one wonders who enjoys them!

Malay food is more problematic for visiting vegetarians as, of the three cuisines available, this is the one that relies most heavily on meat and seafood. Shrimp paste, chicken stock and lard are widely used and several online reports suggest that vegetarians who operate a kind of 'don't ask, don't tell' policy will have a much easier time of it than those who are more determined to stick to their principles. Look for restaurants with English-speaking staff where food is prepared to order and see if you can persuade the chef to do something special for you. Awareness and understanding of vegetarianism received a boost when several politicians 'came out' as vegetarians recently, among them the Malaysian Health Minister Datuk Sri Liow Tiong Lai. He has been given an award by PETA (People for the Ethical Treatment of Animals) in recognition of his work promoting vegetarianism in the country.

Mohana Gill's website is at **fruitastic.net**

The 41st International Vegetarian Union World VegFest and the 6th Asian Vegetarian Congress take place in Kuala Lumpur in October 2013.

MALAYSIA

Vegetable rendang

Although rendang originated in Indonesia, historical literature indicates that it has been a part of Malay cuisine since at least the 1550s – although this reference is to the beef-based dish, not to a vegetarian variety! Indonesian rendang is traditionally a slow-cooked dish, taking hours to prepare as the coconut milk it contains reduces down to a sticky brown state. Malay rendang uses desiccated coconut to thicken the dish, is cooked much more quickly and is golden-yellow in color. It's usually accompanied by steamed rice.

Ingredients

3 tbsp desiccated coconut

2 garlic cloves

6 shallots or 1 onion, sliced

2 stalks lemongrass, trimmed and sliced

2-3 fresh red chilis

2 tbsp fresh ginger, grated

1 tsp turmeric

Salt to taste

1 tsp sugar

1 cup / 250 ml coconut milk

1 tsp tamarind pulp, dissolved in 1 tbsp water

4 star anise

1 inch / 2.5 cm cinnamon stick

2 tbsp fresh cilantro/coriander, plus extra to garnish

10 oz / 300 g firm tofu, or cassava, or any other firm vegetable

Method

Heat a dry frying pan, add the desiccated coconut and toast until lightly golden. Then blend the toasted coconut, garlic, shallots, lemongrass, chilies, ginger, turmeric, salt and sugar together to make an aromatic paste.

Heat some vegetable oil in a heavy-based frying pan. Add the paste and cook for 5 minutes, stirring continuously. Add the coconut milk, along with ½ cup / 125 ml water, the strained tamarind water, star anise and cinnamon and bring to the boil, stirring constantly.

Reduce the heat and simmer gently for a further 5 minutes. Then add the tofu pieces or vegetables and continue to cook gently for another 10 minutes. Stir in the chopped cilantro/coriander. To serve, garnish with more fresh cilantro/coriander.

Terong belado (eggplant/aubergine sambal)

Ingredients

1 large eggplant/aubergine

3 garlic cloves, finely chopped

1 onion, finely chopped

4 fresh tomatoes, finely chopped

2 fresh hot chili peppers, finely chopped

1 tsp sugar

Salt, to taste

½ cup/120ml water

2 tbsp vegetable oil

Method

Preheat the oven to 355°F/180°C. Slice the eggplant/aubergine, lengthways, into quarters. Put it onto a baking tray and bake for 20-25 minutes until soft but not disintegrating.

Mix all the remaining ingredients except the oil together in a bowl, then transfer to a large frying pan and fry gently in the oil until the liquid reduces and the mixture becomes a thick sauce.

Arrange the warm eggplant/aubergine quarters on a serving plate and pour the sauce on top to serve.

MALAYSIA

Bubur pulut hitam (black rice dessert)

Some people don't find this an attractive dish, but I think it looks amazing – a really exotic variant on the good old British rice pudding! I almost wanted to top it with a shred of edible gold leaf. It won't work unless you get proper black glutinous rice, so you'll probably need to visit a specialist shop. Pandan leaves aren't easy to get, but you can substitute a few drops of pandan essence – I bought mine online, and it's worth it for the unusual authentic flavor.

Ingredients

10½ oz / 300 g black glutinous rice

2 pandan / screw pine leaves

1⅓ cups / 200 g caster sugar, or to taste

Coconut milk or coconut cream, to drizzle

Pinch of salt

Method

Wash the glutinous rice thoroughly, cover with water and leave to soak for several hours or overnight.

Rinse the rice and put it into a large pan with 10 cups / 2½ litres of water. Cook over a medium heat until the rice is soft and almost creamy. Stir in the pandan leaves, or essence, and the sugar. Mix well and cook for a further 10-15 minutes. Stir in a pinch of salt. Serve in small bowls topped with 1-2 tablespoons coconut milk or coconut cream.

Mexico

Too often, Mexican food is confused with 'Tex-Mex' food – nachos, chimichangas and burritos are more or less US inventions. But traditional Mexican food is so rich and varied, and so intricately bound up with the country's cultural and social traditions, that in 2010 Mexican cuisine was added to the UNESCO list of 'intangible cultural heritage of humanity', marking the fact that it deserved to be honored and protected.

Mexican cuisine has always benefited from the wide variety of tasty indigenous plants: beans, corn, potatoes, chilis, chocolate, tomatoes, squashes, avocados, vanilla, and all kinds of tropical fruits. The indigenous people relied on a combination of beans and corn for protein, supplemented with occasional meat from small animals and insects. In temperate regions, an ingenious system of companion planting ensured good reliable crops. Beans, squash and corn were planted together – the nitrogen-fixing roots of the beans replenished the soil which would otherwise have become depleted by nitrogen-hungry corn, and the corn provided a trellis for the beans to ramble over. The squash plants covered the soil, keeping the roots of the corn moist. Often, amaranth would complement this arrangement, its graceful grain-laden stems providing shade to help keep the corn from drying out in hot weather. Amaranth grain provided a much-needed source of protein before the corn ripened each year. Sophisticated irrigation systems and calendars also came out of the determination of the people to ensure that crops were reliable.

Historians are not sure how the process of nixtamalization of corn was discovered – without

MENU

Mexican salad in tortilla baskets

•

Tamale pie

•

Avocado ice cream

it, a population reliant on corn as its staple food would soon fall victim to pellagra, a disease caused by vitamin B3 deficiency. By the year 500, the Mexicans had discovered that by treating corn with lime (the mineral, not the fruit), they could make the kernels softer and easier to grind. Previously, corn was used only in stews and gruels. After this development, it became possible to grind corn into a fine flour and to make a dough which in turn yielded the tortillas that are still ubiquitous in the country. The fact that the lime treatment rendered the corn nutritious enough to sustain the population was a very happy coincidence.

The Spanish arrived in Mexico in 1521, and they must have been surprised to see how the Aztecs' sophisticated agricultural systems were sufficient to feed the population. Meat from domesticated animals was unknown, and perhaps this is why the conquistadors suspected that the Aztecs indulged in cannibalism. Historians disagree over whether this was an occasional occurrence linked to religious rituals, or whether human flesh actually formed an important part of the diet – perhaps the Aztecs played up the idea to try to intimidate the Spanish. The Spanish brought cows, pigs, sheep, chicken and goats to the country, for meat. They also introduced dairy products, notably cheese, which had been unknown in Mexico before then. They banned amaranth, probably because it was used in religious ceremonies, and it never really returned to the Mexican table.

Probably the defining feature of Mexican food is the use of chilis – no other cuisine uses more varieties. Although chili sauces were in evidence before the arrival of the Spanish, complicated *moles* (sauces) came later, as ingredients like nuts, seeds, herbs, grapes, garlic, cinnamon and chocolate found their way into the mix. Oaxaca is sometimes called 'The land of seven moles' in recognition of the variety of colorful moles produced there. The use of chilis is the only unifying factor – moles can be black, red, green or yellow, herby or smoky – one well known variety is called *mancha manteles*, which translates as 'tablecloth stainer'!

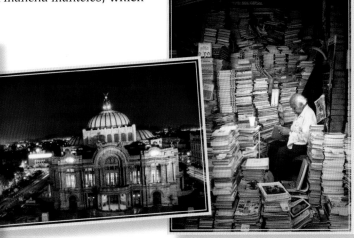

Mexican salad in tortilla baskets

This is one of my favorite dishes in this book – I love how mastering a simple skill like making tortilla baskets can turn an everyday salad into something much more fun. Refried beans add spicy heat as well as boosting the protein content of this dish. You can, of course, make your own, but many recipes suggest using lard or bacon fat – which is traditional in Tex-Mex style cookery, but obviously not suitable for vegetarians. There's no shame in using a can of veggie-friendly ready-made refried beans for a quick and satisfying lunch.

Ingredients

4 large soft tortillas

7 oz / 200 g crisp lettuce, shredded

1 red onion

4-6 scallions/spring onions

1 red bell pepper

1 pound / 450 g canned refried beans

16 ripe cherry tomatoes

1¼ cups / 100g grated cheese

1½ cups / 375 ml guacamole

½ cup / 125 ml sour cream

⅓ cup / 100 g stoned black olives

2 tbsp fresh chopped cilantro/coriander

Method

First, make the tortilla baskets. Preheat the oven to 450°F/230°C. Find a heat-proof bowl that is roughly the same size as you want your tortilla baskets to be. Put it, upside-down, onto a baking sheet and grease it lightly with vegetable oil. Now lay a tortilla over the top of the greased bowl and press it gently but firmly around the bowl, forming a few folds or pleats to bring in the edges. As soon as you take your hand away, it will start to unfurl – that doesn't matter too much, as long as it remains in a basic bowl shape. Pop the baking sheet, bowl and tortilla into the oven and bake for about ten minutes until the tortilla is starting to color. Keep a close eye on it – tortillas are thin and can burn quickly in a hot oven. Retrieve from the oven and allow the tortilla to cool before lifting it off the bowl and setting it upright on a wire rack to cool – it will get crisper as it cools. Continue the process to make four bowls and allow them to cool completely before you use them.

Shred the lettuce. Peel and chop the red onion finely. Trim and chop the spring onions. Deseed and slice the red bell pepper thinly. Cut the tomatoes and olives in half. The refried beans can be served warm or cold.

I like to serve all the salad ingredients in separate little bowls, or in a colorful arrangement on a large serving platter, so that everybody can assemble their own custom-built salads. Simply fill a tortilla bowl with your choice of lettuce, chopped red onion, spring onions, red bell pepper, tomatoes and olives, intersperse some grated cheese, blob on some refried beans, sour cream and guacamole and garnish with cilantro/coriander – or start with a spicy layer of refried beans, it's your call. Serving the food this way means there is no chance for the tortilla baskets to start to get soggy from the salad juices while they are waiting to be eaten.

The Adventurous Vegetarian   **207**

Tamale pie

A colorful stand-alone main course, with a satisfying cornmeal topping hiding a secret layer of gooey melted cheese.

Ingredients

2 onions	1¼ cups / 150 g cornmeal
2 cloves garlic	2 tbsp plain white flour
1 red chili	1½ tsp baking powder
2 tbsp vegetable oil, for frying	½ tsp bicarbonate of soda
2 tsp ground cumin	½ cup / 60 g corn kernels
3½ oz / 100 g green beans	2 oz / 60 g red bell pepper
7 oz / 200 g potatoes	2 tbsp chopped fresh cilantro/coriander
7 oz / 200 g sweet potatoes	2 eggs
1 tbsp lime juice	½ cup / 125 ml milk
1⅓ cups / 100 g grated cheese	2 tbsp vegetable oil, for the pie crust

Method

Preheat the oven to 355°F/180°C.

Peel and finely chop the onions and garlic. Chop the chili finely. Peel the potatoes and sweet potatoes, and cut them into ¾-inch / 1.5-cm cubes. (Precision is not essential!) Trim the green beans and cut into bite-sized lengths.

Heat the vegetable oil in a large, deep saucepan and sauté the onions, garlic and chili together for 2 minutes, then stir in the potatoes, sweet potatoes, cumin and green beans, along with 2 cups / 500 ml of water. Bring the mixture to the boil, then simmer, covered, for 20 minutes until the vegetables are tender.

Stir the lime juice into the cooked vegetables and transfer to a large, deep oven-proof dish.

Chop the red bell pepper finely. Mix the cornmeal, flour, baking powder, bicarbonate of soda, corn kernels, chopped red pepper and fresh cilantro/coriander together thoroughly in a large mixing bowl. Whisk the eggs and milk together with 2 tbsp vegetable oil, then fold the wet mixture into the dry ingredients until just combined.

Cover the vegetables in the dish with the grated cheese, then top with the cornmeal mixture and smooth the top. Bake for 30 minutes until heated through and golden.

MEXICO

Avocado ice cream

Ice cream for grown-ups, this has a rich, creamy texture, a subtle and delicious avocado flavor and show-stopping color.

Ingredients

3 ripe avocados

1 tbsp lime juice

½ cup / 100 g caster sugar

1¼ cups / 300 ml milk

1 cup / 250 ml single cream

Dark chocolate, to decorate (optional)

Method

Peel, stone and mash the avocados roughly, then put all the ingredients into a food processor and blend until completely smooth. You can freeze the mixture right away, but using an ice-cream maker to churn it as it freezes will produce a fabulous creamy texture. A little dark chocolate grated over each serving is an easy but effective finishing touch. Try making chocolate curls by dragging a warm, straight-edged knife along the back of a chocolate bar – it takes some practice, but is a nice skill to have.

New Zealand/ Aotearoa

The Maori migrated to the islands they call Aotearoa ('Land of the long white cloud') from Polynesia and brought with them plants including kumara (sweet potato) and taro. Unfortunately, although the crops grew well in the northern part of North Island, elsewhere it was too cold for them to flourish and so the settlers soon turned to more abundant foodstuffs – grubs, birds and fish. The large, flightless Moa birds were easy prey and quickly hunted to extinction. The arrival of European settlers in the late 18th century brought new crops that thrived in the local climate, including potatoes, pumpkins, wheat and sugar. But with more people to support, the indigenous plants and wildlife were again under pressure and many species, such as the wood pigeon, became scarce. Maori cooking techniques persisted but were supplemented by 19th-century British cuisine, which is still very much in evidence today.

The twin influences of Britain and the Maori culture reigned supreme over New Zealand's food choices until the 1960s and 1970s, when two new influences came into play. First, air travel became affordable and this meant that people from all over the world were able to visit a country which had hitherto been more or less out of reach – and that New Zealanders could see the world. Second, when Britain joined the European Economic Community in 1973, New Zealand could no longer be its chief supplier of agricultural produce (notably lamb). This forced some farmers out of business, and led to others diversifying into new crops or specialty products. The effect was to improve the variety and quality of foods available.

1987 saw the abolition of nationality preferences for immigrants, and the islands saw a surge of arrivals from South and East Asia. Today, New Zealand's cities are home to a high proportion of Thai, Chinese, Japanese and Indian restaurants and food stores. At home, cookery is generally still more like the old-fashioned British settlers' fare (known now as 'Kwisine Kiwiana'), albeit with ingredients and techniques that would have been considered very exotic not so long ago.

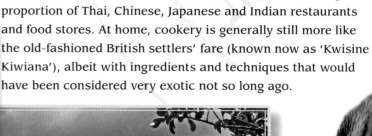

Vegetarianism, although widely accepted as a lifestyle choice, is still relatively rare, with more people dabbling in meat-free eating for the good of their health than going all out for a meat-free diet.

Jeremy Dixon owns and runs two vegetarian cafés in Auckland. He told us:

Much of New Zealand is green pastures used for farming cattle and sheep. Beef, mutton and lamb are still staple foods for many New Zealanders as well as being an important part of the economy, as a great deal of meat is still produced for export. In spite of this, it is not difficult to be a vegetarian in New Zealand. While large quantities of meat dominate most dishes, virtually every restaurant or café will offer at least one token vegetarian dish. Too often this dish is either pasta or a plate of nachos, but we have a lot of ethnic eateries that offer more choice – Indian, Thai and Chinese restaurants often have a lot more on the menu that is suitable for vegetarians or vegans, or can easily be adapted. Most of the main towns and cities have a handful of dedicated vegetarian cafés or restaurants. Again, most of these are based around ethnic eating styles. There are just a few vegetarian establishments in the towns (like the Revive cafes that I run) which offer more exciting European-style vegetarian fare.

We have carried out customer surveys and we know that 80% of our clientele are not vegetarians. I think this goes to show that although New Zealand does not have a lot of vegetarians, more people are choosing meat-free meals more often, mainly for health reasons.

New Zealand Vegetarian Society (**vegetarian.org.nz**).

The following recipes are used with Jeremy Dixon's kind permission and are © Revive Cafés (**revive.co.nz**).

NEW ZEALAND/AOTEAROA

Curried zucchini/ courgette fritters

Ingredients

1 medium onion, finely diced

3 zucchini/courgettes, coarsely grated

1 cup / 100 g chickpea (Gram) flour or wholemeal flour

1 tsp salt

1 tbsp sweet chili sauce

1 tbsp black sesame seeds

1 tsp mild curry powder

Rice bran oil, for frying

Method

Sauté the onion in a little oil until soft and translucent. Mix all the ingredients together in a large bowl. The moisture from the zucchini/courgettes should make everything the right consistency – add a splash of water if it seems too dry to hold together. Let the mixture sit for around 20 minutes in the fridge, then stir again. (If you are in a rush, this is not absolutely necessary, but if you do it you will end up with a more consistent mix that will stick together better.)

Heat a little oil in a non-stick pan and fry small spoonfuls of the mixture for around 4-5 minutes each side or until golden brown and cooked right through. You should have enough mixture for between 10 and 20 fritters. Serve immediately with sweet chili sauce, salsa or chutney on the side.

Shepherdess pie

Ingredients

For the base:

1 cup / 150 g brown lentils

3 cups / 720 ml water

1 large onion, finely diced

1 tsp dried sage

1 tsp salt

2 cups / 450 g passata /
Italian-style tomato sauce

For the topping:

3 large potatoes, steamed and mashed

1 tbsp sweet chili sauce

1 tsp wholegrain mustard

1 tsp ground turmeric

1 tsp salt

1 cup / 240 ml soy or rice milk

Method

Preheat the oven to 300°F/150°C.

Cook the lentils in the water for around 30 minutes or until soft. Drain, if there is any water left. Transfer the lentils to a mixing bowl and mix with the remaining base ingredients.

In another bowl, mix all topping ingredients together.

Put the base mixture into a shallow oven-proof dish, smooth out and top with the potato mixture. Bake for 30 minutes until browning and crisp.

NEW ZEALAND/AOTEAROA

Seedy slaw

Ingredients

2 cups / 225 g finely sliced red cabbage

2 cups / 225 g finely sliced white cabbage

2 cups / 300 g grated carrot

¾ cup / 100 g mixed seeds (pumpkin seeds, sesame seeds, sunflower seeds, poppy seeds)

¼ cup / 15 g chopped parsley

For the dressing:

¼ cup / 60 ml rice bran oil

1 clove garlic, crushed

½ tsp ground cumin

½ tsp salt

2 tbsp lemon juice

Method

Combine the dressing ingredients and mix thoroughly. Put the prepared vegetables, seeds and herbs into a large bowl, toss with the dressing and serve right away.

NEW ZEALAND/AOTEAROA

Blueberry and cashew cheesecake

Ingredients

For the base:

1 cup / 100 g almonds

1 cup / 150 g cashew nuts

1 cup / 150 g dates

For the filling:

2 cups / 300 g cashew nuts

10 pitted dates

¼ teaspoon vanilla essence

Pinch of salt

1 cup / 240 ml boiling water

For the topping:

2 cups frozen blueberries (can be used from frozen)

2 tsp arrowroot (or cornflour)

½ cup cold water

Juice of half a lemon

Method

First, make the base. Soak the dates in half a cup of boiling water for 2 minutes to soften. Drain and place in the bowl of a food processor with the other base ingredients. Process to a clumpy texture – it doesn't need to be smooth. Add a splash of water if the mixture doesn't naturally clump together.

Use a rubber spatula to press the base mixture into a 10-inch / 25-cm tart dish (the ones with the removable bottoms are best). Make sure you form a thick crust around the sides. Now make the filling. Soak the dates in boiling water for 2 minutes, drain them and put them into the bowl of the food processor with the other filling ingredients. Process to a very smooth cashew cream. Pour this into the prepared pie crust and smooth it out.

Now make the topping. Mix the arrowroot into the water, add the lemon juice and pour into a small saucepan. Add the blueberries and heat gently, stirring continuously, until the mixture develops a gel-like consistency. Pour the topping over the cheesecake and use the back of a fork to even it out.

Refrigerate, covered, for several hours to firm up – this makes it easier to slice and serve.

Palestine

Ahmad Safi *is Director of the Palestinian Animal League (PAL) in Ramallah on the West Bank. He writes:*

Being a vegetarian in the Palestinian Territories is a challenge, due to cultural and traditional paradigms that instill human superiority over all creatures and allow and encourage the consumption of animal products. Overcoming this mindset and thinking critically about one's role in ensuring a sustainable world takes strength of mind. Finding alternatives to the cuisine that is densely packed with animal products takes much willpower.

However, those who do choose a vegetarian or vegan lifestyle can enjoy a rich variety of traditional dishes that rely on seasonal vegetables, grains and herbs. This land has a bounty of free-growing foods that are

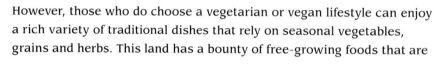

rich in vitamins and minerals, such as wild asparagus, wild hibiscus, arum plants, wild sage and thyme, almonds and walnuts.

I enjoy starting my day with fresh Palestinian flat bread dipped in olive oil and ground thyme. For lunch, there is an assortment of vegetables which may be sautéed and cooked in tomato sauce, followed by a light Mediterranean-style dinner comprising a fresh vegetable salad, toasted flat bread and almonds. Throughout the day I enjoy healthy snacks such as natural almonds and sun-dried raisins, teas with wild mint or sage, and fresh juices.

The Palestinian Animal League (PAL) does not have an office or a website but it does have a presence on Facebook. Ahmad Safi's email address is **ahmad_safi@windowslive.com**

PALESTINE

Stuffed vine leaves

Ingredients

1 pack of vine leaves

3 cups / 450 g long-grain white rice

8 garlic cloves

1½ tsp salt

½ tsp pepper

4 medium tomatoes

Method

Rinse the vine leaves and put them into a large bowl of warm water to soften and unfurl. Slice two of the tomatoes and finely chop the other two. Rinse the rice and mix it with the chopped tomatoes, salt, pepper and crushed garlic.

Lay one vine leaf flat on a board – the veiny bottom of the leaf should be upwards and the tip of the leaf should be furthest from you. Place a teaspoonful of the rice mixture in the center of the leaf. Fold in the sides of the leaf and then roll it up tightly from the base to the tip. Continue until all your leaves and/or stuffing are used up.

Place the sliced tomatoes in the base of a large saucepan, sprinkle with salt and pepper, and arrange the stuffed vine leaves on top. Press them down with your hand and then pour warm water over the dish until your hand is nearly submerged. Put the saucepan on to the hob and heat until the water reaches boiling point, then cover and simmer gently until the water has almost entirely gone – about 25 minutes. Carefully lift the vine leaves out of the pan, arrange on a serving plate and serve hot or cold.

PALESTINE

Imjadara
(rice, lentils and onions)

Mixtures of cooked rice and lentils, topped with fried onions, are enjoyed across the Middle East and Africa. I'm always surprised by how tasty this simple combination can be! Ahmad Safi writes: 'This is my favorite recipe – it's great for lunch or dinner, with an assortment of side dishes such as finely chopped salad and soya yoghurt.' Combinations of grains and pulses are excellent sources of protein for vegetarians and vegans.

Ingredients

3 cups / 450 g long-grain white rice

2½ cups / 450 g brown lentils

1 tsp salt

Black pepper, to taste

3 large onions

Vegetable oil, for frying

Method

Soak the rice in warm water for around 15 minutes. Put the lentils into a large saucepan, cover with water, add half the salt, bring to the boil and then simmer, covered, for 20 minutes.

Chop the onions coarsely and fry them in the oil until they are browned. It's important to let them get quite deeply colored as this is what gives the dish its flavor.

Drain the rice and the lentils and transfer them to a large saucepan. Add half the cooked onions, the rest of the salt and some black pepper. Cover with water – the surface of the water should be about 5cm higher than the surface of the rice and lentils. Bring to the boil, cover and simmer gently for about 20 minutes until the rice is cooked and there is little or no water remaining in the pan. Transfer to a serving platter and garnish with the remaining onions.

Barazek (sesame cookies)

There are many variations on this theme – one side of the cookies is covered with sesame seeds, but the other side might be plain, or covered with chopped pistachios, hazelnuts or any combination of nuts and seeds. Presentation boxes and celebration platters generally include several different varieties. It's important to roll the cookie dough thinly so that it cooks quickly – otherwise the nuts on the base can burn. This recipe uses egg replacer and is suitable for vegans. There are many different brands of egg replacer available – you will need to add water to the powder before you use it (follow the instructions on the packet).

Ingredients

1 cup / 230 g soft vegan margarine

2/3 cup / 120 g caster sugar

4 fl oz / 110ml reconstituted egg replacer, plus extra for brushing

½ tsp vanilla essence

3⅓ cups / 330 g plain white flour

¼ tsp salt

1 tsp baking powder

½ cup / 120 ml soya milk

3 tbsp chopped pistachios

3 tbsp sesame seeds

Method

Preheat the oven to 355°F/180°C. Cream the margarine and sugar together, and beat in the egg replacer and vanilla. Mix the flour, salt and baking powder together and gradually add these to the mixture, alternating with splashes of soya milk, to make a dough that is soft but not too sticky to roll out. Roll it out thinly on a floured board and use a cookie cutter to cut out circles. It's fine to re-roll the trimmings. Put the chopped pistachios onto a plate. Press one cookie at a time into the nuts so that each one picks up a few, then transfer, nutty side down, to a baking tray lined with parchment. Brush the tops of the cookies with the remaining egg replacer and sprinkle generously with the sesame seeds. Bake for 12-15 minutes until just golden.

Russia

The old Soviet Union is the only country, to my knowledge, to have actually banned vegetarianism. Vegetarian groups were forced 'underground' after the revolution of 1917, and were actively persecuted, ironically partly because of their adherence to the principles of nonviolence. Vegetarianism was deemed to be unscientific and bourgeois. There is also a possibility that the ruling Communist Party suspected that groups of counter-revolutionaries were meeting to plot against the state, and using vegetarianism as a convenient excuse to hide their real purpose – and they may have been right. As recently as 1961, the 'Big Soviet Encyclopedia' was absolutely dismissive: 'Vegetarianism is based on false hypothesis and ideas and has no followers in the Soviet Union'. The word was removed from Soviet dictionaries.

Had it not been for this, vegetarianism in Russia might today be as advanced and accepted as it is in other parts of Europe. The movement was certainly enjoying a period of growth immediately before 1917, with a vegetarian journal, *First Step*, operating in St Petersburg in the 1890s, and St Petersburg Vegetarian Society launching in 1901, followed by a group in Kiev in 1908 and one in Moscow in 1909. Vegetarian dining halls, hospitals and magazines mushroomed. One of the greatest driving forces behind the growth of vegetarianism was Count Leo Tolstoy, who insisted that the first principle of ethical living was 'Thou shalt not kill', and that this must apply to animals as well as to humans. In April 1913, the First All-Russia Vegetarian Congress took place in Moscow.

It attracted support from all kinds of notables – writers, composers, academics, scientists, painters and sportspeople.

Interest in vegetarianism had deep roots in Russian Orthodox Christianity, with 14th-century saints preaching that true belief in God was incompatible with meat-eating. The Lenten diet, followed by Orthodox Russians for more than 220 days of the year, banned meat, eggs and dairy food. Fish with backbones were not allowed, but some sea creatures such as crabs and prawns were considered permissible. Olive oil and wine were generally not included in the Lenten diet, but were permitted on certain celebration days and on Saturdays and Sundays. It's easy to see how people familiar with dietary restrictions of this kind found it straightforward to embrace vegetarianism.

After 1917, vegetarianism remained more or less underground until 1989 and 'perestroika', when a new Vegetarian Society was formed by a group of doctors and ethical scientists. The Eurasian Vegetarian Society (**vege.ru**) launched in 2001 and several of the ex-Soviet states have small but active vegetarian groups (such as the Vegetarian Union of Moldova, **uvem.org**).

While it remains quite difficult to obtain a vegetarian meal in a Russian restaurant, cities like Moscow are home to a wide variety of eateries offering cuisine from around the world. Most will be familiar to the adventurous vegetarian but Georgian restaurants are hard to come by outside the old Soviet Bloc, and Georgian cuisine offers relatively good pickings for vegetarians.

RUSSIA

Lenten mushroom soup

A swirl of sour cream would be delicious in a bowl of this soup, but strictly speaking, a Lenten soup must be dairy-free... if you're not observing Lent, the choice is yours!

Ingredients

2 onions

1 cup / 30 g dried mushrooms
(a mixture of varieties is fine)

2 tbsp vegetable oil

12 cups / 900 g fresh button or
chestnut mushrooms

2 carrots

2 potatoes

2 leeks

2 cloves garlic

6¼ cups / 1.5 litres vegetable stock

2 tbsp chopped fresh parsley

Method

Soak the dried mushrooms in hot water for 10 minutes, then drain, rinse and chop. Peel and dice the onions, carrots, potatoes and leeks. Peel and crush the garlic. Wipe and slice the fresh mushrooms.

In a deep saucepan, fry the onion gently in the vegetable oil until golden brown. Add the leeks and garlic and cook gently for a further 5 minutes. Add the fresh mushrooms and cook on a low heat, uncovered, for 15 minutes – the mushrooms will release some water and this will gradually reduce away.

Add the rehydrated mushrooms, all the remaining vegetables and the stock to the pan. Simmer, covered, for around 40 minutes, until all the vegetables are tender. Allow the soup to cool a little and then liquidize, in batches. It's nice to leave some of the soup unprocessed so that the finished soup still has some distinctive flecks of color and texture. Reheat and stir in the parsley before serving.

RUSSIA

Red bean pkhali

Pkhalis originated in Georgia but variants are enjoyed across the former Soviet Union. The hallmark of the dish is always the combination of ground walnuts, garlic and herbs. Presenting the mixture rolled into little balls means you can eat them whole, as part of a buffet, or crush them on bread as a light lunch. I love them with the warm cheesebread that follows.

Ingredients

1 cup / 1 can (400 g) aduki beans

1 cup / 100 g walnut pieces

2 cloves garlic

1 stick of celery

A handful of fresh, finely chopped cilantro/coriander

½ tsp ground fenugreek

½ tsp ground coriander

A handful of fresh pomegranate kernels

Method

Chop the walnuts, celery and garlic finely. Drain and rinse the beans. Mash the beans with the walnuts, garlic, celery, cilantro/coriander and spices. Roll the mixture into bite-sized balls, top each with a pomegranate kernel and refrigerate for 30 minutes before serving.

Khachapuri (cheese bread)

Another delight from Georgia, enjoyed across the region. This bread with its salty stuffing of feta and mozzarella is best straight out of the pan. The soft, smooth dough enriched with yoghurt is easy to handle and the technique is not difficult – but the results are impressive.

Ingredients

2¼ cups / 225 g plain white flour (or try a mixture of white and brown bread flours)

3 tbsp vegetable oil

¾ cup / 180 ml plain yoghurt

1 tbsp cornflour

1 tsp bicarbonate of soda

⅓ cup / 50 g feta cheese

½ cup / 100 g mozzarella cheese

1 egg

Method

In a large bowl, mix the flour, cornflour and bicarbonate of soda together. Stir in the vegetable oil and yoghurt and use your hands to mix it to a soft dough. Cover the bowl with a clean dishcloth and leave to rest at room temperature for an hour or two. Grate the mozzarella and break up the feta. Beat the egg. Mash the cheeses and the egg together and set aside.

Divide the dough into two equal portions and roll each into a ball. Place on a floured surface and roll into a circle about ¼ inch / ½ cm thick. Put half of the cheese mixture into the center of the dough circle. Lift the outer edges of the dough up around the cheese and squeeze the edges together to seal the cheese inside the dough. Gently pat the bread into a flattened circle. Repeat with the remaining dough and cheese. Heat a heavy-bottomed frying pan or a cast iron skillet and when warm, coat the base with a little butter. Put the bread into the pan, seam-side up. Reduce the heat to a bare minimum and cook the bread for around 10 minutes on each side. Serve warm, sliced into wedges.

RUSSIA

Medivnyk (honey cake)

Honey cakes and pastries of all kinds are popular around Christmas time – at one time sugar was scarce and families experimented to make sweet treats in other ways. Like most honey-based cakes, the flavors of this cake become richer when it has been stored for a few days – wrap it in greaseproof paper and store in an airtight tin.

Ingredients

½ cup / 125 ml runny honey

½ tsp cinnamon

½ tsp ground cloves

½ tsp ground nutmeg

²/₃ cup / 90 g mixed currants and raisins

¹/₃ cup / 50 g dates, chopped

½ cup / 75g walnuts, chopped

¼ cup / 25g plain white flour

½ tsp baking powder

1 tsp bicarbonate of soda

Pinch of salt

¼ cup / 55 g butter, softened

¾ cup / 80 g brown sugar

2 eggs

¹/₈ cup / 30 ml strong black coffee

Method

Preheat the oven to 300°F/150°C. Grease a loaf tin.

Put the honey into a small saucepan with the spices, bring to the boil, then take off the heat and set aside.

Put the dried fruit and nuts into a bowl and mix with a tablespoon of the flour. Put the remaining flour, baking powder, bicarbonate of soda and salt into a large mixing bowl and mix well.

Cream the butter and sugar together. Separate the eggs and beat the yolks into the butter and sugar mixture. Stir in the honey, then gradually add the flour mixture and the coffee, alternating so that the mixture never becomes too stiff to work with.

Stir in the fruit and nuts. Whisk the egg whites to soft peaks and fold them into the cake mixture. Gently spoon the mixture into the prepared tin and bake for approximately 90 minutes until a skewer inserted into the centre of the cake comes out clean.

Singapore

These recipes were contributed by Shalu Asnani, a cooking instructor, private chef and food consultant based in Singapore. Shalu came to the project via George Jacobs, President of the Vegetarian Society Singapore – their informative website, **vegetarian-society.org**, includes more recipes and useful tips for vegetarians and vegans visiting the country. Shalu runs **littlegreencafe.com.sg**, a vegetarian cooking site that provides inspiration for fantastic vegetarian cuisine and healthy eating tips. Shalu is a self-taught chef who left the corporate world to pursue her real passion of cooking and teaching people to be healthy. She writes:

'Being vegetarian is relatively easy in Singapore. We enjoy a variety of cuisine, including Indian, Malaysian, Chinese and unique Singaporean dishes. Singaporeans in general eat a lot of vegetables and tofu as part of their diet, so it's easy to

MENU

Tofu satays

•

Peanut sauce

•

Mee goreng
(noodles with tofu)

•

Pandan coconut
pancakes

get vegetarian food when you dine out. Sometimes you need to be specific and remind them not to add any fish sauce or "belacan" (shrimp paste), but most restaurants and even hawker stalls are pretty accommodating. It also helps to get creative by asking them to make something that's not on the menu and offering ideas on what they can substitute with! Overall, the vegetarian diet is well-respected as Singaporeans are becoming increasingly conscious of health and environmental issues and of the need to understand the consequences of the food choices they make.'

To attend one of Shalu's creative cooking classes or to hire her as your personal chef/food consultant, visit the website or email **shalu@littlegreencafe.com.sg**

You can also follow Little Green Café on Facebook to get free recipes and other useful tips.

SINGAPORE

Tofu satays

Ingredients

2 blocks of firm tofu

1 red bell pepper

1 yellow bell pepper

1 onion

12 cherry tomatoes

1 clove garlic, very finely chopped

1 tsp salt

1 tsp ground cumin

1 tsp ground coriander

1 tsp chili powder

2 tbsp vegetable oil

Satay sticks

2 tbsp lemon juice

Method

Chop the tofu into 1-inch / 2.5-cm cubes and pan-fry in a little vegetable oil until light golden brown. Chop the peppers and onions into bite-sized pieces.

Make the marinade: mix the garlic, salt, ground cumin, ground coriander, chili powder and vegetable oil.

Place the chopped peppers, onion, tomatoes and tofu on a large plate and pour the marinade over them. Mix well and set aside to absorb the flavors for approximately an hour.

Soak the satay sticks in water for 30 minutes – this will help to prevent them from burning when you cook the satays. Skewer the vegetables and tofu on the sticks and cook, either on a barbecue or under a hot grill, turning regularly, for around 20 minutes until slightly charred. Serve with peanut sauce (see page 242).

SINGAPORE

Peanut sauce

Kecap manis is a sweet soy sauce widely available in both specialist shops and supermarkets.

Ingredients

1⅓ cups / 200 g raw, unsalted peanuts (with skin)

1 tbsp palm sugar or brown sugar

Salt to taste

2 shallots, sliced and fried

3 cloves garlic, very finely chopped

1-2 red chilis, finely chopped

1 tomato, peeled and chopped

1 cup / 250 ml warm water

2 tbsp kecap manis

2 tbsp lime juice

2 fresh lime leaves, finely shredded (optional)

Method

Fry the peanuts in a little vegetable oil, a handful at a time, and remove with a slotted spoon. Grind them with the sugar, salt and fried shallots. If using a food processor, you may need to add a bit of water, and take care not to blend the mixture too long – it should still have a crunchy texture. Mash the garlic, chilis, tomato, salt and sugar into a paste. Mix this with the ground peanuts. Add the warm water, kecap manis and lime juice. Taste and adjust seasonings. Just before serving alongside the satays, stir in the lime leaves (if available).

Mee goreng (noodles with tofu)

Ingredients

1 block of firm tofu, sliced into thin strips

3-4 tbsp vegetable oil

2 cloves garlic, very finely chopped

3 shallots, chopped

½ leek or 2 scallions/spring onions, finely chopped

1 large red chili, chopped

½ carrot, julienned

4-5 baby bok choi, chopped

½ pound / 225 g soft yellow noodles

2 tbsp kecap manis (see opposite)

2 tsp soy sauce

1 tbsp tomato ketchup or tomato paste

Salt to taste

Fried shallots for garnish

Method

Heat the oil in a wok and pan fry the tofu strips until golden brown. Add the garlic and shallots, and stir-fry for a moment or two, then add the leeks or scallions/spring onions, red chilli, carrot and bok choi. Mix thoroughly, tossing around to prevent it sticking to the wok.

Add the noodles, followed by the sauces and salt. Mix and toss. Keep tossing until the vegetables are cooked to your taste. Garnish with fried shallots to serve.

The Adventurous Vegetarian **243**

Pandan coconut pancakes

Pandan essence is a bright green liquid made from the leaves of the pandanus palm, or screwpine. It's well worth seeking out this special ingredient, in Asian cookshops or via the internet, as it has a unique flowery flavor that makes these pancakes authentic. If you can't obtain fresh coconut, or don't want to go to the trouble of cracking a coconut and grating the flesh, you can use desiccated coconut to make the filling for these pancakes – cover it with coconut milk and leave to soak for 15 minutes, then squeeze out the excess milk and continue with the recipe.

Ingredients

Pancake batter:

⅔ cup / 60 g plain flour

½ tsp salt

½ tsp vanilla essence

½ tsp pandan essence

1 cup / 250 ml water

2 tbsp sugar

½ cup / 125 ml coconut milk

1 tbsp lemon juice

Filling:

1⅓ cups / 100 g grated fresh coconut

1 tsp pandan essence

½ tsp vanilla essence

5 tbsp palm sugar

Pinch of salt

Oil or butter for frying

Icing sugar for dusting

Method

Whisk all the pancake ingredients together but do not add all the water in one go; add in stages until you get a smooth and lump-free batter. Set aside and make the filling.

Mix all the filling ingredients together and cook over low heat for a few minutes until the coconut is soft.

Heat a frying pan and add a smear of oil, followed by 2 tbsp of pancake batter, tilting the pan so that it reaches the edges. The pancake should be quite thin. When bubbles appear, flip the pancake and cook on the other side. Add a smear of butter or oil whenever necessary, using a pastry brush. Continue until mixture is finished.

Fill each pancake with 2 tbsp of coconut filling and roll like a spring roll, starting with the sides and rolling tightly from bottom up.

Serve warm with a dusting of icing sugar.

Tanzania

Tanzania was formed in 1964 by the unification of Tanganyika, which is part of mainland East Africa, and Zanzibar, a group of islands in the Indian Ocean. Although the mainland area has borders with Kenya, Uganda, Rwanda and Burundi to the north and west, and Zambia, Malawi and Mozambique to the south, it's notable that a lot of the edges of the country are defined by three of Africa's Great Lakes – Malawi, Victoria and Tanganyika. Fish from the lakes and the sea play a prominent role in the nation's diet. Today, Tanzania is home to 43 million people, from more than 120 different ethnic groups. The mainland is divided along religious lines, with 35% of the population Muslim, 30% Christian and the remainder following a variety of different traditional faiths. Zanzibar, in contrast, is 99% Muslim. The people of Tanzania are not big meat-eaters but tend to base meals around fish, with occasional chicken and duck meat. A soft polenta-style cornmeal mixture called *ugali* is enjoyed daily in many homes, served with spicy sauces and eaten with the fingers from a communal bowl.

The Zanzibar archipelago has been called The Spice Islands because of its production of cloves, nutmeg, cinnamon and black pepper. Although the importance of this trade has now diminished, in the 19th century the impressive scale of production was recognized worldwide – and the fact that the spices were grown on plantations worked by slaves was also well known. Zanzibar's cuisine reflects a history of colonization and invasion, with traditional African dishes of fish, beans, sweet potatoes, coconuts, bananas and plantains sitting alongside fragrant spiced Arabic rice pilaus. Today's staples, manioc and maize, were brought in by Portuguese conquerors in the 15th and 16th centuries.

In 1651 the Omani Sultanate took control of Zanzibar, bringing Indian-style dishes like samosas, chutneys and curries. The early 20th century saw most of East Africa ruled by Germany and Britain, but there is little evidence of this in the cuisine, as the Germans and British apparently failed to socialize with the rest of the island's inhabitants.

In the early 1960s, Tanzania's independence leader Julius Nyerere announced his vision of an African form of socialism that would include *ujamaa* – collective farms that would revolutionize the country's agricultural productivity. Sadly, it had the opposite effect, with many inhabitants of small farming communities resistant to change and eventually forcibly resettled. Nyerere's successors have pursued policies more in tune with the free-market orthodoxy, including exploitation of minerals and tourism. Tanzania remains, however, primarily an agricultural society; many people are subsistence farmers, while others work on plantations growing tea and coffee, cotton, cashew nuts and tobacco for export.

Vegetable soup with bananas

This hearty soup is close to being a stew, as it is crammed with vegetables. The shredded red cabbage creates a stunning purple color in the dish, and peanut butter adds body and protein. Canned chopped tomatoes are acceptable if the prospect of all this chopping is off-putting!

Ingredients

1 onion

8 cups / 2 litres vegetable stock

1 tsp ground ginger

1 tsp ground cinnamon

1 tsp ground cumin

Cayenne pepper, to taste

10 oz / 300 g tomatoes, chopped

1 pound / 450 g potatoes

1¾ cups / 225 g sweetcorn kernels

8 oz / 225 g carrots

8 oz / 225 g red cabbage

150 g / 5 oz green beans

2½ oz / 75 g peanut butter

1 banana

3 tbsp chopped roasted peanuts

Method

Peel and dice the potatoes and carrots.

Peel and chop the onion. Cook it in ½ cup / 125 ml of the vegetable stock, in a large saucepan, for 5 minutes until it has softened. Stir in the spices, chopped tomatoes, sweetcorn, carrots and potatoes, and the rest of the vegetable stock. Bring to the boil, then simmer, covered, for 25-30 minutes until all the vegetables are tender.

Shred the red cabbage and chop the green beans into short lengths. Add these to the pan. Mix the peanut butter with ½ cup / 125 ml of boiling water and stir it into the soup. Simmer for a further 15 minutes until the cabbage is cooked. Garnish each bowlful with chopped banana and peanuts.

TANZANIA

Squash and sweet potato futari

A simple, delicate-tasting, traditional stew. It's not a curry, but you could pep it up with some chili or cayenne if you need more of a kick.

Ingredients

1 pound / 450 g butternut squash

1 pound / 450 g sweet potatoes

1 onion

1 cup / 250 ml coconut milk

1 tbsp vegetable oil

1 tsp ground cinnamon

½ tsp ground cloves

Salt, to taste

Method

Peel the squash and sweet potatoes and chop into small chunks. Peel and finely chop the onion.

Heat the oil in a large, deep pan and fry the onion gently for 2-3 minutes. Stir in all the remaining ingredients, bring the mixture to the boil and then reduce the heat and simmer, covered, stirring occasionally, until the vegetables are tender (approximately 15 minutes, depending on the size of the pieces). Serve hot with rice or polenta.

TANZANIA

Kashata (Swahili sweet peanut snack)

A popular Swahili snack which can be made with peanuts, shredded coconut or a mixture of the two. Sometimes flour is stirred into the mix to give it a slightly more biscuity consistency – use ½ cup / 50 g of plain flour if you want to try it that way. Without the flour, or the coconut, it's like a very chunky, spiced peanut brittle – which seems to go down very well whenever it is served.

Ingredients

2 cups / 400 g white sugar

1¾ cups / 300 g roasted peanuts

½ tsp cloves

½ tsp cinnamon

½ tsp ground cardamom

A pinch of salt

Method

Put the sugar into a large frying pan and heat it until it dissolves. When it is just beginning to caramelize, take it off the heat and quickly stir in the remaining ingredients. It's important to work quickly – don't let the sugar burn, as the taste will be horrible. As soon as you add the nuts and spices, the temperature of the sugar will fall and it will go from being a runny syrup to a much thicker, stickier consistency. You may need help – somebody to hold the pan while you stir. As soon as everything is combined, spread the mixture out on a large sheet of baking parchment. Let it cool completely, then break it up into manageable chunks. If you're feeding guests, serve it with a cup of chai.

Chai (sweet spiced tea)

Some chai recipes require you to make a spiced syrup, or infuse the milk with whole spices and then add it to tea – but I like this quick all-in-one method.

Ingredients

4 cups / 1 litre water

4 cups / 1 litre milk

4 tsp black tea leaves

1 tsp ground cardamom

1 tsp ground ginger

Sugar, to taste

Method

Heat all the ingredients together in a large pan. Bring them to boiling point, then simmer gently for a few minutes. Strain, and serve hot.

Thailand

Thai food is light and full of fresh flavors. Coconut milk is used in many dishes, both sweet and savory, along with chilis, lime, tamarind and fresh herbs like lemongrass and Thai basil. Creating a balance of sweet, sour, salty and bitter flavors is important, and Thais love their food to be complex, with many elements contributing to the whole. The recipe on page 256 for *miang* is a perfect demonstration of this – a combination of finely chopped shallots, ginger, lime, tomatoes, cashews, lemongrass, hot chilis and sweet-sour tamarind sauce, all wrapped together in a bite-sized parcel.

The cuisine of the country is influenced by the fact that it is home to more than 40 distinct ethnic groups, each with their own favorite ingredients and ways of preparing food. The neighboring countries of China, Vietnam and Malaysia have also contributed culinary influences. Interestingly, there is an important influence from the West, too: when King Chulalongkorn returned from a tour of Europe in 1897, the royal court switched from the usual hand-to-mouth way of eating and began to use forks and spoons. Today, eating directly from the hand is no longer the norm, except when sticky rice is served, when small, flattened balls of rice are often used to scoop up food. Otherwise, a fork is used to push food into a spoon and then brought to the mouth. Traditional ceramic spoons may be used for eating soups – but chopsticks are not used, other than for eating noodle soups.

The West remained largely oblivious to Thai cuisine until the 1960s, when US troops fighting the Vietnam war arrived in the country in large numbers. Their positive reports about the beautiful country and tasty food stimulated an influx of Western tourists, and then a rush to open Thai restaurants in the US and Europe. Surveys purporting to reveal the world's favorite dishes regularly rate Thai food very highly, and its popularity has spawned

MENU

Miang
(Thai veggie bites)
•
Pad Thai
•
Sticky rice with mango

a new tourist market, with visitors to the country enjoying culinary tours and cookery classes.

Sadly, the Thai food served in Thailand poses problems for vegetarians because of the ubiquitous use of seafood products like fish sauce and shrimp paste, which fill the role of salt in many dishes. Thai Buddhists are not necessarily vegetarians: Theravada Buddhism prohibits the slaughter of an animal specifically to feed a Buddhist, but permits them to accept food of any kind, including meat, if it is offered as alms. There are, however, specialist restaurants that adhere to stricter Buddhist ideas, where the food is vegan and also excludes certain strong-tasting spices and vegetables. These restaurants are marked by a sign: the word *che* written in red, on a yellow background. Otherwise, the best vegetarian-friendly food is likely to be found at Indian-style restaurants run by Hindu Thai-Indians.

Thailand has a very active vegetarian organization, the Thai Vegetarian Association (TVA), which in 2012 hosted the 5th Southeast Asian Vegetarian Congress, in collaboration with the Southeast Asian Vegetarian Union (SEAVU) in Chiang Mai. The TVA's president, Dr Maitree Suttajit, put me in touch with Duang Dhanapume Asoke-trakul, a chef who runs a vegetarian restaurant in Chiang Mai. A vegetarian for over 20 years, Duang started his career as a food stylist and consultant for new restaurants, helping them to design menus and honing their presentation. He has written four cookbooks and is now working on an English-language collection of his recipes. His Brown Rice organic bistro in downtown Chiang Mai serves Thai and Western-style vegetarian food. The bistro has a busy Facebook page. I have adapted Duang's recipes very slightly to take account of the availability of ingredients.

THAILAND

Miang (Thai veggie bites)

Duang translated Miang as 'Veggie bite' – a bite-sized appetizer packed with flavorful ingredients, chopped finely and wrapped in a crisp lettuce leaf. If you can't find tamarind juice, buy a block of pressed tamarind, let it soak in a little boiling water, then mash it with a fork until it breaks down. Put the pulp through a sieve to get your tangy, smooth tamarind juice. Palm sugar has a distinctive taste but can be a little gritty – good quality brown sugar is a reasonable substitute.

Ingredients

2 small crisp lettuce hearts
   (such as 'Little Gem')

1 pack of firm tofu (approx ⅔ pound / 300 g)

Vegetable oil, for frying

⅓ cup / 55 g cashew nuts

2 shallots

1-inch / 2.5-cm piece of fresh ginger

1 lime

1 stalk fresh lemongrass

4 cherry tomatoes

2 fresh bird's eye chilis

For the Tamarind sauce:

1 cup / 250 ml tamarind juice

1 cup / 200 g palm sugar

½ cup / 125 ml soy sauce

Method

Drain the tofu, pat it dry with a paper towel and chop it into small dice. Shallow-fry in a little vegetable oil until crisp, then drain and set aside. Dry roast the cashews in a heavy-bottomed pan for a minute or two until they begin to brown, then tip them onto a cool plate to halt the cooking.

Make the tamarind sauce by heating all the ingredients together over a medium heat. Stir thoroughly until the sugar has dissolved and the sauce is bubbling, then set aside to cool.

Peel and finely dice the shallots, ginger and lime. Trim and finely slice the lemongrass. Chop the tomatoes into very small pieces. Chop the chili very finely – large pieces can be an unwelcome surprise as bird's eye chilis are often very hot.

Trim the base of the lettuce hearts and separate into individual leaves.

Arrange the leaves on a serving plate and then carefully place a little of each of the filling items into each leaf. Drizzle the filled leaves with tamarind sauce and serve the rest of the sauce in a small shallow bowl for dipping. To eat, simply pick up a filled leaf, using your fingers to fold it up around the filling, and pop it into your mouth whole. Be ready for an explosion of flavors!

THAILAND

Pad Thai

The most popular noodle dish in Thailand. Duang garnishes his with an egg 'net' – have a go, it's fun and impressive to create. His original recipe also included a tablespoon of chopped salted turnip, which should be fried along with the tofu and shallot at the beginning of the cooking process.

This recipe calls for tamarind sauce – check the recipe for Miang on page 256 for directions on making this.

Ingredients

3½ oz / 100 g Thai rice noodles

½ cup / 55 g beansprouts

2 Chinese chives or scallions/spring onions

3½ oz / 100 g firm tofu

1 shallot

½ cup / 125 ml tamarind sauce

1 egg

1 tbsp ground roasted peanuts

Chili powder, to taste

A piece of lime, to taste

2 tbsp vegetable oil

Method

Make the omelet net first. Brush a large, heavy frying pan with vegetable oil and set it over a low heat. Beat the egg thoroughly. Drizzle the beaten egg into the warm pan. There are utensils designed specifically for this job but with a bit of practice you can get an impressive effect by letting the beaten egg run off a spoon, and quickly moving the spoon from side to side over the pan, to create a net. You won't need to use all the egg – save what is left, you will need it later. The 'net' will cook almost instantly – the trick is to stop it from getting too crisp and brown by sliding it out of the pan and onto some kitchen towel as soon as it has firmed up – no need to attempt to turn it over! Set it aside to cool.

Peel and finely slice the shallot. Drain the tofu, pat it dry with some kitchen paper and chop it into bite-sized pieces. Heat the remaining cooking oil in a wok, and gently stir-fry the tofu and shallot for 2 minutes. Add the noodles and ½ cup / 125 ml boiling water. Stir in the tamarind sauce and cook the noodles gently until the moisture has almost gone.

Trim the Chinese chives or scallions/spring onions. Chop the white part, and set it to one side. Cut the green part into short lengths.

When the noodles are almost dry, stir in the remaining beaten egg, the beansprouts and the green parts of the Chinese chives or scallions/spring onions. Stir everything together quickly and then remove from the heat.

Pile the Pad Thai onto a serving dish and cover it with the omelet net. Garnish the edge of the plate with the chopped white parts of the Chinese chives or scallions/spring onions, chili powder, fine slices of lime and ground roasted peanuts.

THAILAND

Sticky rice with mango

Duang describes this as the best, and most well-known, dessert from Thailand. Split dried mung beans look like tiny yellow lentils – the green skins of the beans are discarded. They have a sweet, floury taste and add an interesting crunchy garnish to the soft, sticky rice. Coconut cream isn't the same as creamed coconut. Coconut cream is just like coconut milk, but with a bit less water in the mix. Creamed coconut is a solid block of dehydrated coconut flesh that has been ground to a smooth paste. Just to confuse things further, you may also find 'Cream of Coconut' – this is a sweetened coconut cream mainly used to make pina coladas and other cocktails.

Ingredients

7 oz / 200 g uncooked Thai sticky rice

3 cups / 750 ml coconut cream

¼ cup / 50 g white sugar

4 tsp salt

4 tbsp split mung beans

2-3 ripe mangoes

Method

Soak the sticky rice in water for four hours.

While that's happening, make your coconut sauce. Put 2 cups / 500 ml of the coconut cream into a small saucepan, stir in two teaspoons of the salt and simmer over a medium heat until bubbling. Remove from the heat and set aside to cool.

Prepare the split mung beans by roasting them gently in a dry pan until they are golden. Set aside to cool.

Drain the rice and rinse it until the water runs clear. Then put it into a steamer and steam it for 20 minutes until it is sticky and tender.

Mix the remaining ½ cup / 125 ml of coconut cream with the sugar and remaining salt. Stir thoroughly to dissolve the sugar.

Put the hot sticky rice into a large mixing bowl and gently mix in the sweetened coconut cream. Cover the bowl and let the rice sit for 10 minutes, then stir it again and leave it, covered, for a further 10 minutes.

Peel, stone and chop the mango.

To serve, divide the rice between four serving plates and give each a portion of mango on the side. Dress with a spoonful or two of the coconut sauce and sprinkle with crunchy roasted mung beans.

Togo

Erick Mokafo-Brhom Yeleneke, the President of the Vegan Students' Association of Lomé, Togo and an active member of the International Vegetarian Union (IVU), made contact to offer some recipes. His report on the Togo Association's work, with photos, is on the IVU's website at ivu.org/africa/togo/index.html

Erick writes: *On 20 March, the International "Meat Out" day, we went out to tell our fellow students that we are in the golden age already because we have the choice to become what we want. The young people of Africa need to learn to take care of their health in order to become truly useful citizens. We cooked some soya kebabs and walked around the university all day, offering free food to everybody. All the students and even some university authorities who tried the kebabs said it was fantastic to have such alternative food. Many students asked us to teach them how to cook vegan food.*

In the Cultural Week that followed, we organized cookery demonstrations and showed them how to use soy and gluten meat alternatives. Soy milk, vegetarian seasonings, dried mushrooms and black mushrooms were among many vegan products we displayed. We made the vegan kebabs and showed students how to make vegan mayonnaise using cooked potatoes, soy milk, mashed garlic, oil and salt. People from all races rushed to our stand to get the food and more information about veganism (how to begin, where to buy vegan products, how to cook them, the relationship between vegetarianism and climate change and what we humans should do to curb the ills of global warming).

We got our financial aid from a student and former president of the Vegan Students' Association who went to China for his Doctorate studies. We respect the IVU a lot because we got inspiration from its Congress in Ghana. We want to work harder but we are students and most of the time we lack financial support. We know a lot of hard times but we will never stop. We will fight as hard as we can.

Togo was a German colony from the late 1880s until the end of the First World War, when it was divided and given to the French and British. The country was reunited and gained independence in 1960. Despite its long history of European rule (and use of the French language), the people of Togo saw no reason to change their culinary traditions. Protein is mainly provided by fish and bush meat, especially giant rats, known as 'grass cutters'. The land is fertile, and staples include maize (predominantly), millet, cassava, plantains, yams, rice and beans. Fufu, a dense paste traditionally made from pounded cassava, is also made with yams, millet, plantains and even instant mashed potato. Typically it is served with rich spicy sauces made with meat or smoked fish, and patés made from ground peanuts or cassava.

Making fufu the traditional way is a communal task, with the strongest people in the community taking turns to pound starchy vegetables with a hefty stick. The resulting dough is formed into balls and eaten with the hands. The dense, putty-like texture means that it is inadvisable to chew it. Although it's possible to make something approximating traditional fufu using a food processor, there comes a point when it's better to provide a recipe that is 'inspired' by traditional cuisine, rather than giving directions to make something that is very much an acquired taste! I thought Western home cooks would get more enjoyment out of a variation on the traditional *ugali*, another thick paste, this time made with cornmeal.

TOGO

Papaya salad

Choose a papaya and tomatoes that are not over-ripe – for this recipe, they're best if they're firm and slightly tart.

Ingredients

1 papaya

3 tomatoes

½ cup / 60 g sweetcorn kernels

One or two sprigs of fresh mint

2 tbsp olive oil

Juice of 1 lemon

Method

Peel the papaya, cut it in half and scrape out and discard the seeds. Grate it using the coarsest holes on your grater. Chop the tomatoes roughly. Strip the mint leaves off the woody stems, discard the stems and chop the leaves finely. Stir all the ingredients together and chill before serving.

TOGO

Togo tofu with baked ugali

I've taken some liberties in transforming *poulet djenkoumé*, a very popular chicken dish, into a vegan feast. It's not traditional, but it is delicious.

Ingredients

1 pack firm tofu (approx 14 oz / 400 g)

Vegetable oil, for frying

For the tomato sauce:

4 scallions/spring onions

4 onions

3 cloves garlic

2 chilis

3 tbsp tomato paste/purée

3 tbsp olive oil

4 tomatoes

For the stock:

4 cups / 1 litre vegetable stock

3 cloves garlic

1 inch / 2.5 cm root ginger

For the baked ugali:

1¼ cups / 200 g polenta

2 tbsp tomato paste/purée

A little vegan margarine

Method

Peel and roughly chop the garlic, ginger and scallions/spring onions. Put them into a saucepan with the stock, and cook on a low heat for 10 minutes.

Drain the tofu, pat it dry with kitchen paper and cut it into 8 substantial pieces. Arrange the tofu pieces in a layer in the base of a deep dish. Pour the hot stock, with the pieces of garlic, ginger and scallion/spring onion, over the tofu and leave it to marinade for at least an hour (or overnight).

Gently remove the tofu from the marinade and set to one side on a plate. Pass the stock through a sieve and discard the solids. Reserve the strained stock.

Peel and coarsely chop the onions. Peel and chop the garlic, and chop it finely. Deseed and chop the chilis. Gently fry the onions, garlic and chilis in the olive oil for 5 minutes, until the onions are soft and translucent. Stir in the tomato paste/purée and 5 tablespoons of the reserved stock. Chop the tomatoes finely and stir them into the mixture. Then add the tofu, stir gently so that the tofu pieces are covered with the tomato sauce, turn off the heat and put a lid on the pan.

Preheat the oven to 355°F/180°C, then grease and line a baking tray.

Make the reserved stock up to 3¹/₃ cups / 800 ml, and stir in the tomato paste/purée. Pour it into a saucepan and bring it to the boil. Add the polenta in a steady stream, whisking continually. Cook on a low heat, still stirring continuously, for 3-4 minutes until it is very thick and bubbling volcanically. Pour the polenta into the prepared baking tray, smooth the top and dot with vegan margarine. Bake for 20 minutes until golden and then cut into 8 regular pieces.

Take the tofu pieces out of the tomato sauce – don't wipe off the excess sauce. Shallow-fry them gently, turning to crisp up each side. Reheat the tomato sauce. To serve, place two pieces of polenta on each serving plate, place a piece of fried tofu on each piece of polenta and finish with a blob of tomato sauce.

TOGO

Black bananas

I love the drama of this dish – the perfectly black banana skin peels back to reveal bright yellow fruit. Choose bananas that are ripe but not going brown.

Ingredients

4 large bananas

4 tsp brown sugar

4 tsp lime juice

½ cup / 125 ml cream or vegan cream

A handful of chopped roasted peanuts

Method

Preheat the oven to 355°F/180°C. Put the bananas, whole, onto a baking sheet and bake them for 20 minutes, until the skins are black. To serve, peel a strip of the skin back to reveal the yellow flesh, and garnish with the chopped nuts, lime juice, sugar and cream. Or bring a show-stopping bunch of hot blackened bananas to the table and serve all the toppings in little bowls for everybody to help themselves.

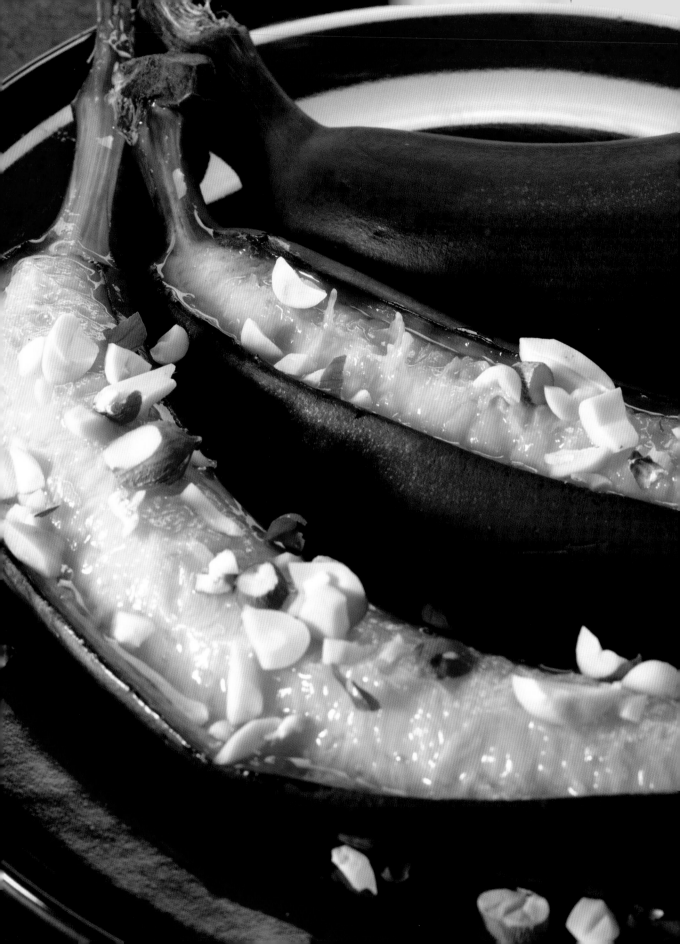

United States

A study commissioned by the US magazine *Vegetarian Times*, carried out by Harris Interactive in 2008, concluded that around 7.3 million Americans (3.2% of the population) were vegetarians, with 22.8 million more (10% of the population) following what they considered to be a 'vegetarian-inclined' diet. Paradoxically, although the typical American diet is widely considered to be the epitome of the unhealthy Western-style pattern of eating that's blamed for high rates of obesity, heart disease and other self-induced illnesses – and although Americans are world-renowned for eating exceptionally large portions of meat – US organizations such as PETA (People for the Ethical Treatment of Animals) are world leaders when it comes to campaigning to get people to go vegetarian or vegan.

This may be a country where eating meat is considered an act of patriotism, and where cowboys, ranchers and rustlers play a revered role in the nation's history, but it's also easy, today, to see the impact that industrial-scale meat production and consumption is having, not just on the environment but also on people's health. Most American vegetarians and near-vegetarians have changed their diet for health reasons, with environmental concerns cited as a close second consideration. Vegans, though still a minority within the US vegetarian movement (0.5% of the total population according to the 2008 survey), are increasingly vocal campaigners, arguing that a plant-based diet, excluding dairy products as well as meat, is the healthiest, most ecologically responsible and most ethically sound choice available.

Colleen O'Brien, communications director for PETA US, supplied the recipes for these salads and the chocolate tart. She writes about her experience of being a vegan in the US:

Thanks to the rising number of vegetarians and vegans, finding vegan food in the US has become as easy as pie. My job with PETA is based in Washington DC, and I regularly travel to our offices in Norfolk, Virginia, and Los Angeles, and to special events in New York City. All

four cities are teeming with spectacular vegan
food. In Washington, my favorite is the vegan
grilled cheese with tempeh bacon at Sticky Fingers,
but the baked manicotti at Everlasting Life Café and
the vegan meatloaf at Café Green are not to be missed.
There are also are some top-notch Ethiopian, Chinese, and
Thai restaurants with several vegan dishes to choose from. In
Norfolk, I never miss the teriyaki 'chicken' with rice at Kotobuki. Los
Angeles is a virtual mecca for vegan food, but I'd have to rate the seitan (wheat protein) tacos at
Real Food Daily as my number one choice. And in New York, it's straight to the famous, upscale
Candle 79 for its seitan piccata. When I eat at restaurants in smaller cities and towns, I've found
that the wait staff and cooks will go out of their way to accommodate me.

If I get a craving for "down home" American comfort food, I can always order a veggie burger,
tofu chili, or wheat-based fried 'chicken', or if I'm at home I can whip up some macaroni and
'cheese' – an American staple – using nutritional yeast and vegan cheese. Most grocery stores carry
whatever type of food I'm in the mood for – or the ingredients I need to make it – so I'll make a kale
salad if I'm feeling health-conscious and, if I have more time, I'll cook my favorite vegan lasagne
recipe.

I originally stopped eating meat because it's the most effective way to help stop animal suffering, but
it's also great for my health. Vegans get all the protein and other nutrients that they need but without
the artery-clogging cholesterol and saturated animal fat. When I stopped eating dairy products, I
noticed an immediate boost in my energy level. Also, as in all industrialized nations, water pollution,
land degradation, and greenhouse-gas emissions are big problems in the US, and meat, dairy, and egg
production are major contributors to these environmental ills. For people who care about animals,
their health, and the Earth, eating vegan food makes perfect sense.

UNITED STATES

Kale salad

A substantial meal in itself, this nutritious salad is rich in vitamins from the raw green and orange vegetables, as well as protein and omega-3 from the walnuts. Nutritional yeast flakes are a great addition to a vegan diet – they have a cheesy taste and are rich in B-vitamins. Some brands contain additional vitamin B12, which is of special interest to vegans who need to obtain this vitamin in their diet through fortified foods.

Ingredients

- 1 bunch of kale (approximately eight large leaves)
- 5 carrots
- 5 celery stalks
- 1 orange bell pepper
- 1 cup / 100 g walnuts
- 1 avocado
- 1 tsp balsamic vinegar
- 2 tbsp extra virgin olive oil
- 2 tbsp nutritional yeast flakes
- Salt and black pepper

Method

Remove the stalks from the kale and chop the leaves into small pieces. Mix the chopped kale with the olive oil and then mix in the balsamic vinegar. Add 1 tbsp salt and 1 tbsp pepper. Chop the carrots, celery and orange bell pepper into small pieces and mix them into the salad. Peel, stone and chop the avocado, and stir it into the salad along with the walnuts. Finally, sprinkle on the nutritional yeast and toss it through the dish.

Tangy black bean and corn salad

Ingredients

- 1 pound / 450 g canned black beans, rinsed and drained
- ¾ cup / 100 g fresh or frozen corn kernels
- 1 avocado, peeled, stoned and diced
- 1 red bell pepper, diced
- 2 tomatoes, diced
- 6 scallions/spring onions, chopped very finely
- 2 tbsp chopped fresh cilantro/coriander
- Juice of 1 lime
- ½ cup / 120 ml olive oil
- 1 clove garlic, chopped very finely
- 1 tsp salt
- a pinch of cayenne pepper

Method

In a salad bowl, combine the beans, corn, avocado, bell pepper, tomatoes, scallions/spring onions and cilantro/coriander. Place the lime juice, olive oil, garlic, salt and cayenne pepper into a small jar. Cover with a lid and shake to mix thoroughly, then pour over the salad ingredients and stir gently to coat. Serve immediately or refrigerate for later, stirring again before serving.

UNITED STATES

Vegan mac'n'cheez

Macaroni and cheese is classic American comfort food – and something that many US vegans have tried to veganize, with varying results! The latest developments in vegan cheese substitutes make the job easy – but many varieties of vegan 'cheez' are still not easy to obtain outside the US. This recipe relies on nutritional yeast flakes to deliver a satisfying cheesy taste.

Ingredients

11 oz / 300 g dried macaroni

⅔ cup / 125 g vegan margarine

⅔ cup / 60 g plain white flour

½ pint / 1 litre boiling water

½ tsp salt

2 tbsp soy sauce

2 cloves garlic, peeled and finely chopped

A pinch of turmeric

¼ cup / 60 ml vegetable oil

1 cup / 50 g nutritional yeast flakes

A dusting of smoked paprika

Method

Preheat the oven to 345°F/175°C. Cook the macaroni in boiling water until just tender, drain and set aside. Melt the margarine in a saucepan, stir in the flour and cook for a minute, stirring constantly. Whisk in the boiling water, salt, garlic and turmeric, and continue to stir until the mixture thickens. Then add the oil and nutritional yeast flakes, mix thoroughly and remove from the heat.

Stir around three-quarters of the sauce into the macaroni and transfer to a deep oven-proof dish. Pour the remaining sauce over the top and sprinkle with a little smoked paprika. Place the dish in the oven to warm through (around 15 minutes), and, if you like, pop it under a hot grill to brown the top just before serving.

Chocolate tart

Ingredients

For the crust:

½ cup / 100 g vegan margarine

⅓ cup / 80 g sugar

1 tsp vanilla

¼ cup / 30 g walnuts, finely chopped

1½ cups / 150 g plain white flour

For the filling:

6 oz / 175 g dark chocolate, chopped

1¼ cups / 300 ml strong black coffee

2 tbsp cornflour

1 tsp vanilla

pinch of salt

¾ cup / 75 g slivered almonds (optional)

Method

Preheat oven to 355°F/180°C. Cream the margarine and sugar together, then add the vanilla and walnuts and mix well. Add the flour, a little at a time, and mix until the dough sticks together and is slightly moist.

Press the soft dough into a tart pan with your fingertips, forming a smooth crust without any holes. Bake until the edges are just barely starting to brown, about 20 minutes. Allow the crust to cool completely before filling.

For the filling, melt the chocolate. Bring the coffee to boiling point, pour onto the warm chocolate and stir until smooth. Mix the cornflour with a little water to make a smooth paste, then stir into the warm chocolate with the vanilla and salt. Pour the filling into the cooled pie crust and refrigerate the pie for at least 6 hours. Decorate with slivered almonds (optional), slice and serve.

Vietnam

Vietnamese cuisine is fast gaining a devoted following in the West. Food plays an important role in Vietnamese culture, and meals are carefully balanced, taking into account the principles of Yin and Yang, five tastes (spicy, sweet, sour, bitter and salty), five colors (white, green, red, black and yellow), five senses and five 'nutrients' (protein, fat, mineral elements, powder and liquid). The cuisine relies heavily on fresh herbs and vegetables, minimal oil and carefully selected spices. While it is often said to be one of the world's healthiest styles of food, Vietnam has also won some notoriety amongst vegetarians and vegans because of the willingness of its people to eat things that most others would consider revolting. Poverty, long periods of war and political insecurity have fostered a culture in which no food is wasted and the Vietnamese happily consume offal, blood sausage, and the feet, testicles, tails, skin, faces and brains of animals.

This book is not the place to go into more detail – although unwary vegetarians would do well to avoid a street-food breakfast favorite called *balut* or *hot vit lon*, a fertilized duck egg containing a well-developed fetus which is boiled and eaten from the shell. Vietnamese street food is certainly not for the squeamish. The ubiquitous fermented raw fish sauce (*nuroc mam*) also presents problems for vegetarian visitors.

The cuisine's strong-flavored salty and fishy sauces have developed to help make the cheapest food palatable. Happily, tofu, fresh raw vegetables and a wide variety of sweet pastries (a legacy of French colonial times) are available to help feed vegetarians.

The recipe on page 282 for *pho*, a traditional northern Vietnamese noodle dish, was shared by Duyen Nguyen Thi Bao and Paul Tarrant of Karma Waters, a vegan restaurant in Hoi An (**karmawaters.com**). Although Pho traditionally contains beef, tripe or chicken, there is a strong history of a vegetarian version known as Pho Chay, which was developed to suit Buddhist vegetarians. Chay means meat-free and visitors to the country will find Pho Chay at both Buddhist temples and restaurants. There is a difference between the dishes, however, as food prepared to the strictest Buddhist principles cannot include root vegetables (as to eat these involves killing the plant), or certain strong-smelling plants including onions and coriander. This can mean that the food served at the temples is rather bland. Restaurants often interpret the rules far more loosely and even if a dish is called Pho Chay, it might be made with non-vegetarian ingredients, so be sure to check before you jump in!

VIETNAM

Goi cuon
(Vietnamese spring rolls)

Ingredients

1 carrot

4 scallions/spring onions

1 red pepper

A handful of fresh beansprouts

1 tbsp mint

1 tbsp parsley

1 tbsp mirin*

1 tbsp sesame oil

10 small rice paper wrappers

> * Mirin is a form of rice wine commonly used as a condiment, in East Asian, especially Japanese, cooking.

Method

Peel and grate the carrot. Trim and finely chop the scallions/spring onions. Deseed the red bell pepper and cut it into fine slices. Chop the fresh herbs finely and mix all the filling ingredients together in a large mixing bowl.

Prepare a large bowl of water – about the temperature you would use to do the washing up. Cover your work surface with a clean, dry kitchen cloth.

Place one rice paper wrapper in the warm water and leave it for just a few seconds, until it is flexible but not completely soggy. This can take a bit of practice! Lay the soaked wrapper on the cloth and place a generous teaspoon of the filling near to the edge closest to you. Fold the two sides of the wrapper in so that they just overlap the filling, then carefully lift the edge closest to you and fold it over the filling. Continue to roll the spring roll away from you as tightly as you can, and then transfer to a serving plate, seam down. Continue with the remaining wrappers and serve the spring rolls, whole or sliced, with a sweet chili dipping sauce.

VIETNAM

Pho (stir-fried noodles)

Ingredients

1 lb / 450 g thin flat dried rice noodles

1 onion

14 oz / 400g firm tofu

2-3 handfuls of mushrooms

4 vegan sausages

4 tbsp vegetable oil

4 cloves garlic

A 'thumb' of ginger

1 pack fresh beansprouts

Fresh coriander and basil

4 tbsp mushroom sauce

Salt and black pepper

2 litres vegetable stock

½ tsp ground cardamom

½ tsp ground aniseed

½ tsp ground cinnamon

Method

Peel and chop the onion. Peel and finely chop the ginger and garlic. Wipe and trim the mushrooms, and slice them. Drain the tofu, then use paper towels gently to press out excess water. Cut the tofu into cubes around ¾ inch / 2 cm square. Cut the vegan sausages in half, lengthways, and fry them in a little oil until cooked.

Soak the noodles in hot water until they begin to soften, then drain, refresh under cold running water, drain again and set aside.

Heat the oil in a large pan or wok. Stir-fry the garlic, ginger and spices for 30 seconds, then add the mushrooms, onion and tofu. Stir-fry for a minute or two, then pour in the mushroom sauce and vegetable stock. Bring to the boil, then reduce the heat to simmer the mixture. Adjust the seasoning to your taste with salt and pepper. Add the noodles to the pan, mix well and cook gently for 5-10 minutes until everything is soft.

Rinse the beansprouts and divide them between four serving bowls. Spoon the noodles on top, followed by the 'soup' that remains in the pot. Garnish with the sausage slices, fresh cilantro/coriander and basil, and serve with hot chili sauce and soy sauce.

VIETNAM

Che kho
(mung bean pudding)

These sweet, dainty cakes are traditionally served during Vietnamese Lunar New Year (Tet) celebrations (usually calculated to fall on the same day as Chinese New Year). The celebration marks the arrival of Spring, according to the lunar calendar.

Ingredients

1½ cups / 250 g split peeled mung beans

1¼ cups / 250 g granulated sugar

1 tsp vanilla extract

3 tbsp sesame seeds

Method

Cover the mung beans with water in a large pan, bring to the boil and then simmer until the beans are soft. Top up the water if you really need to, but bear in mind that the next stage is to drain away as much of the water as you can! When you have cooked and drained the beans, transfer them to a food processor and whizz them into a smooth paste. Return them to the pan and stir in the sugar and vanilla. Put the pan onto a low heat and cook the mixture, stirring constantly, until the sugar melts into the beans and the paste is very thick and smooth. You should barely be able to stir it. Divide the mixture between 6 small plates or saucers, press down firmly and smooth the tops.

Roast the sesame seeds in a dry pan until they begin to change color, then sprinkle them over the puddings and set aside to chill until needed. Serve in wedges with a glass of green tea.

Photo Credits

All recipe photography by Graham Alder/MM Studios

Photographs on the country introduction pages are used under a Creative Commons Attribution License. They are credited left to right as they appear on each country spread. Where one photo is more prominent and does not fit the left-right axis, it is described in brackets. Postage stamps are not credited.

Australia: Simon Loffler; Dick Tay; Simon Loffler; Aussiegall; Mike Baird.
Belgium: Ian Nixon; Ian Nixon; Josef Stuefer; albrechtpaul; Ian Nixon.
Botswana: Graham Alder, SqueakyMarmot, Mara1, Jon Rawlinson
Brazil: seier+seier; babasteve; eflon; (owl) WagnerMachadoCarlosLames; Laszlo-photo; Diego3336.
Canada: Cindy Andrie; Graham Alder; Melissa Bowman; yurilong.
Chile: Iniue_FJ; Saavedra; (bird) Volar_Fenanov; Dave_B; alvazer; francisco_osorio.
China: Graham Alder; yakobusan; ChiKing; yakobusan; kevinpoh; (police) BeijingPatrol.
Cuba: Alex Barth, cmrlee, Leshaines123
Denmark: seier+seier; Mikkel Rask; seier+seier; Tiws;jimg.
Egypt: Bakar; Muhammad Ghafari; JKM; John Thomas; Heather Cowper.
England: All Ian Nixon.
Ethiopia: babasteve; A Davey; A Davey; AhrondeLeeuw; AhrondeLeeuw.
France: All Ian Nixon.
Ghana: paulinuk; 300td; Stig Nygaard; Muse1inspired; Stig Nygaard; Dredrk.
Grenada: Sun Cat; Paul Lowry; Lee Edwin Coursey; Alex Barth; Jason Pratt.
India: mckaysavage; Vinoth Chandar; Vinoth Chandar; Amy Hall; (bee eater bird) Vinoth Chandar; Vinoth Chandar.
Ireland: UggBoy; Bachmont; Amy Hall; UggBoy, Sarcasticalious; Rowan of Ravara.
Israel: (cats) miss pupik; bachmont; david55king; Ilan's Photos; amira_a; Edoardo Costa.
Lebanon: (cedar tree) Ahmed Sager; rabiem22; Andreas Kollmorgen; rabiem22; raibem22.
Malaysia: Mohammed Alnaser, Terence S Jones: Terence S Jones: MVI; Tallkev.
Mexico: uteart; Eneas; sebpaquet; Eneas; Eneas.
New Zealand/Aotearoa: Jenny Huang; Church_Phillip; Tony Fischer; PaullBica; ???.
Palestine: (main pic of Hebron children) David Masters; dlisbona; gnuckx; hoyasmeg; upyernoz.
Russia: Michael Gwyther-Jones; Anton Novoselov; geeazweezer; mksystem; Anton Novoselov.
Singapore: (spider) givozaid85; notsogoodphotography; ???; notsogoodphotography; Swami_Stream.
Tanzania: wwarby; Stig Nygaard; wwarby; Irene2005; frontierofficial.
Thailand: (food) Thaijasmine; DearTerisa; Mike Behnken; puulibench; ????.
Togo: (dove statue) Jeff Attaway; Julius; Erik Cleves Kristensen; geezaweezer; 300td.org.
United States: (crane flying) Tscherno; Ken Zirkel; TonyFischerPhotography; conner395; Loli; OliBac.
Vietnam: Irargerich; hktang; Carrie Kellenberger; Greg Hayter; Erik Charlton.

Index

Index

Index

Index

Index

Index